The Saint and Greavsie Football Book

Ian St John and Jimmy Greaves

Edited by Bob Patience

Illustrations by Jake Tebbit

Stanley Paul

London Melbourne Auckland Johannesburg

First published in 1987 by Stanley Paul & Co. Ltd.

An imprint of Century Hutchinson Ltd

Brookmount House, 62–65 Chandos Place
Covent Garden, London WC2N 4NW

Century Hutchinson Australia (Pty) Ltd
PO Box 496, 16–22 Church Street, Hawthorn, Melbourne,
Victoria 3122

Century Hutchinson New Zealand Limited
191 Archers Road, PO Box 40–086, Glenfield, Auckland 10

Century Hutchinson South Africa (Pty) Ltd
PO Box 337, Bergvlei 2012, South Africa

Set by Avocet Marketing Services, Bicester, Oxon.

Printed and bound in Great Britain by
Anchor Brendon Ltd, Tiptree, Essex

British Library Cataloguing in Publication Data
St John, Ian
The Saint and Greavsie football book.
1. Soccer
I. Title   II. Greaves, Jimmy   III. Patience, Bob
796.334   GV943

ISBN 0 09 173456 8

Contents

Acknowledgements

Thanks are due to Barry Roberts for the Temple of Gloom, Jake Tebbit for the black and white illustrations, Chris Rhys for compiling the sports quiz and to the following for allowing the use of copyright photographs:

Black and white: AllSport, Colorsport, London Weekend Television, The Photo Source, Sport and General Press Agency, Sporting Pictures (UK) Ltd, Syndication International

Colour: AllSport, Colorsport, Sport and General Press Agency, Sporting Pictures (UK) Ltd

1

A funny old year

Ian and Jimmy

Season 1986–7 was an eventful one in British football. Unusual happenings, surprise winners, shock sackings, play-offs and massive transfers plus the European Championships. This opening chapter reflects on the good, the bad and the funny sides of soccer ... with a few thoughts on it all by Saint and Greavsie.

1986–7 Season

Pre-season news and transfers

British football loses the talents of Mark Hughes and Gary Lineker who join Terry Venables at Barcelona in multi-million pound deals.... Ian Rush signs a £3 million deal with Juventus, but is to stay at Anfield until the end of the season.... Arsenal's Tony Woodcock returns to Cologne in a £200,000 deal.

SAINT: *At this rate, Greavsie, the only strikers left in this country will be biscuits*

At home, some big pre-season signings include Garry Thompson from Sheffield Wednesday to Aston Villa for £450,000.... England 'keeper Chris Woods goes north of the border to Rangers from Norwich for £600,000.... Bournemouth's Northern Ireland striker Colin Clarke moves along the south coast to Southampton for £400,000 .... England international Terry Butcher joins Chris Woods at Rangers: the fee £700,000.... Liverpool pay Sunderland £200,000 for full back Barry Venison, while neighbours Everton buy England defender Dave Watson from Norwich City for £900,000.... England Under-21 'keeper David Seaman moves from Birmingham to QPR for £250,000.... After missing out on Terry Butcher, Spurs pay Dundee United £750,000 for defender Richard Gough.

Wolves, Middlesbrough, Gillingham and Swansea all fight off winding-up orders and start the season, while Walsall stay put at Fellows Park, despite plans to play at St

Andrews, home of Birmingham City.... Bert Millichip re-elected as chairman of the FA.... The Scottish FA make the shock announcement that the new national team manager will be Andy Roxburgh, a man without previous club management experience.... The football world is saddened by the death of Sir Stanley Rous, one of the game's great administrators and innovators. Sir Stanley was 91.... Justin Fashanu is advised to quit by Brighton because of a recurring knee injury.

On the managerial 'merry-go-round' ex-player Brian Miller succeeds Tommy Cavanagh at Burnley, and Terry Yorath quits Bradford City to take charge at Swansea.

And so to the start of the season

August

9th

The Scottish season starts.... Celtic beat Dundee 1-0 but Rangers lose 2-1 at Hibernian. It is a sad start to Graeme Souness' new career as Rangers' player–manager – he is sent off.

10th

Gary Lineker breaks a rib playing for Barcelona.

11th

Boardroom unrest at Sunderland. Chairman Tom Cowie, the man who brought Lawrie McMenemy to Roker, resigns and sells all his shares.... Sheffield Wednesday pay Barnsley £250,000 for David Hirst even though he has played only 28 League games.

GREAVSIE: *And that was only to pay Big Lawrie a week's wages*

13th

Celtic and Aberdeen both win in the Scottish Premier Division, while an Ally McCoist penalty gives Rangers a 1-0 win over Falkirk.

14th

With just nine days to the start of the English season, there is a chance Middlesbrough will not be lining up for their opening fixture. Last-minute moves to save the club continue.

15th

Sammy Chapman dismissed as Wolves manager – by the Official Receiver. All members of the staff sacked except the players!

16th

Everton and Liverpool draw 1-1 in the Charity Shield in front of 88,000 at Wembley. Everton open the scoring shortly after Bruce Grobbelaar goes off with a stomach injury and is replaced by Mike Hooper – Grobbelaar's first replacement in five years. Ian Rush equalizes for Liverpool.... In Scotland Rangers fall four points behind Celtic after a 3-2 home defeat by Dundee United. The near-capacity 44,000 crowd greets Souness with chants of 'What a load of rubbish' towards the end.

SAINT: *Least said Souness mended*

19th
Southampton sign 17-year-old Matthew Le Tissier, from Guernsey: he is the first Channel Islander for nearly 30 years to join a League club.... Ex-Villa and England striker Brian Little appointed manager of Wolves.... Scottish FA fines Rangers £5,000 and bans Graeme Souness for three matches.

20th
The FA offers Bobby Robson a new five-year contract, keeping him until 1991.... Dennis Mortimer, the man who captained Aston Villa to their European Cup triumph, joins Birmingham on a free transfer from Brighton.

GREAVSIE: *A big hand for Bobby – and I don't mean Maradona's*

21st
Birmingham sign Steve Whitton from West Ham for £75,000.... Sheffield Wednesday full back Peter Shirtliff moves to Charlton for £125,000 and makes his Charlton debut against Wednesday.

23rd
The opening day of the season.... Ian Rush opens his account after five minutes in Liverpool's 2–0 win at Newcastle.... Everton also win 2–0, at home to Nottingham Forest.... Attendances slightly up, but not at Halifax – only 1,020 turn up at the Shay for the visit of Aldershot.... Middlesbrough make the start of the season but play their opening home game against Port Vale at Hartlepool's ground.... Wimbledon's First Division baptism ends in a 3–1 defeat at Maine Road.... Colin Clarke scores a hat-trick on his Southampton debut in 5–1 defeat of QPR.

25th
Liverpool held at home by Manchester City in 0–0 draw.... Manchester United lose 3–2 at home to West Ham. Frank McAvennie scores two goals for the Hammers.... Everton draw 2–2 at Sheffield Wednesday.... Sammy Lee leaves Liverpool and joins QPR for £200,000.

26th
Wimbledon have first-ever win in top flight, beating Aston Villa 3–2 at Plough Lane.... QPR find winning touch, beating Watford 3–2 at Loftus Road.... Sunderland lose at home 4–2 to York City in the 1st round of the Littlewoods Cup.... Cardiff put five goals past newly promoted Plymouth to win 5–4 in their first-round match.

27th
Neil Webb scores two goals in Forest's 4–0 win over Charlton in the First Division.

28th
Arsenal's David O'Leary left out of Republic of Ireland squad for first time in more than 10 years.

SAINT: *A case of one, two and out O'Leary?*

30th
Tottenham, Liverpool and West Ham set pace in First Division, with seven points each.... Liverpool beat Arsenal 2–1 at Anfield, thanks to goals from Jan Molby and Rush.... A Graham Roberts goal gives Spurs a 1–0 win over Manchester City, and West Ham are amongst the leaders after a goalless draw at Oxford.... Manchester United lose again, their third successive defeat, this time 1–0 at home to Charlton.... Wimbledon beat Leicester 1–0 and lurk one

point behind the leaders.... In Spain, Gary Lineker scores both Barcelona's goals on his League debut for the club.

31st

Rangers, without Souness, beat Celtic 1-0 in the Glasgow derby in front of 43,502 fans. The only goal of the game comes from Iain Durrant midway through the second half.

GREAVSIE: *Does that mean Schnozzle-nosed Rangers ahead?*

September

1st

Ray Stewart recalled to Scotland squad, four years after he last wore a Scottish shirt.

2nd

Everton beat Oxford 3-1 to challenge at the top of the table, but the new leaders are Wimbledon after their 1-0 win at Charlton. Dennis Wise scores the historic goal.... Oldham top of the Second Division after beating Ipswich 1-0 at Portman Road.... In the Littlewoods Cup, Sunderland look like pulling back and winning at York when they lead 3-0 with a minute to go, then Keith Walwyn scores to put the home team through on the away goals rule.... Everton's Kevin Richardson joins Watford for £225,000.

SAINT: *Wimbledon are just wild about 'Harry' – Dave Bassett*

3rd

Liverpool lose their first game since February when beaten 2-1 at Leicester.... QPR recover from their disastrous start to the season by beating Newcastle 2-0.

4th

George Graham completes his first signing as Arsenal manager by buying Perry Groves from Colchester.... Cardiff City, drawn to meet Luton in the 2nd round of the Littlewoods Cup, incensed by their plan to ban away supporters, appeal to the Football League to allow their fans to take up their 25 per cent ticket allocation.

6th

Wimbledon remain top of the First Division with 1-0 win at Watford. Glyn Hodges does the damage in the 89th minute.... Two goals from manager Kenny Dalglish help Liverpool to a 5-2 win at West Ham while Everton drop a point at home to QPR in a 1-1 draw.... Arsenal and Spurs derby ends up goalless, and Manchester United collect their first point of the season by drawing 1-1 at Leicester. They remain bottom of the table.... Middlesbrough, who have only just started the season, top the Third Division by beating Bury 3-1.

GREAVSIE: *Atko worried – pawns first ring*

7th

Glyn Hodges, whose goal keeps Wimbledon top, is called into the Welsh squad.

9th

England Under-21s draw 1-1 with their Swedish counterparts. A member of the team is Aston Villa's Tony Dorigo who, it is discovered, holds an Italian passport and, consequently, his international career could be in jeopardy.... Crystal Palace, who had their boots stolen earlier in the week, beat Huddersfield 1-0 at Selhurst Park, to go second to Oldham.

SAINT: *They should play in their bare feet every week!*

10th

England, missing Gary Lineker, are beaten 1-0 by Sweden in a friendly in Stockholm .... Scotland draw 0-0 with Bulgaria at Hampden in the European Championship and Liam Brady scores a last-minute penalty to earn a 2-2 draw for the Republic of Ireland in Belgium. In group six Wales draw 1-1 in Finland.

11th

Former Luton Town manager 'Happy' Harry Haslam dies at the age of 65.

12th

Swansea, another club who faced possible winding-up before the start of the season, emulate Middlesbrough and go top of the Fourth Division after a fine 2-1 win at Southend United.

13th

Wimbledon face their toughest test yet, and lose 2-1 at home to Everton, the only unbeaten team in the top division. The defeat means Nottingham Forest top the table after 6-0 massacre of Aston Villa. Liverpool and Everton fill second and third places.... Liverpool beat Charlton 2-0 thanks to Molby and Rush goals.... Success at last for Manchester United. They beat Southampton 5-1 to register their first win of the season.... Spurs rocked by a couple of Micky Hazard goals as Chelsea win 3-1 at White Hart Lane.... In Scotland Dundee United remain unbeaten and top the Premier Division after a magnificent 2-2 draw with Celtic, while Rangers show continued improvement with a 4-0 win over Clydebank.... After their defeat by Forest, Villa sack manager Graham Turner.

GREAVSIE: *Deadly Doug strikes again*

14th

Northampton beat Peterborough 2-1 to top the Fourth Division.

15th

Kenny Dalglish causes a stir on Merseyside by refusing injury-torn Everton permission to play new signing Dave Watson in the 1st leg of the Screensport Super Cup Final carried over from last season. Although the rules state a player must not play for two teams in the competition in one season, this is now another season ... confused?

SAINT: *So was Howard Kendall*

16th

Two Ian Rush goals help give Liverpool a 3-1 lead in the Screensport Cup in front of a mere 20,000 fans.... Manchester United's revival dented by Ian Roberts who scores the only goal of the game for Watford at Vicarage Road.... Bournemouth beat Chester 2-0 to become new leaders in Division Three while Preston are new leaders in Division Four.... Tom Devlin, Celtic's chairman, dies on eve of their European campaign.

17th

The start of the European campaign: in the European Cup Celtic win 1-0 against Shamrock Rovers and Linfield lose by the same score at Rosenborg.... Wrexham win 3-0 away from home, against Zurrieq of Malta, in the Cup Winners' Cup, while Aberdeen just scrape home 2-1 against little-known Sion of Switzerland.... Robert Fleck scores a hat-trick for Rangers in the UEFA Cup against Tampere of Finland as Rangers win the 1st leg 4-0.... Hearts beat Dukla Prague 3-2 in the UEFA Cup.

18th

Peter Shilton dismisses rumours linking him with the Aston Villa manager's job.

19th

Journalist and former chairman of the Football Writers' Association, Peter Lorenzo, dies suddenly at the age of 59.... Oswestry Town thrown out of the FA Cup competition for fielding a player under an assumed name in the 1-0 win over Prescot Cables. The player, real name Steve Austin, appeared as Andy Cross. He played for another team four days before the tie, thus contravening FA Cup rules.

GREAVSIE: *The headline: Oswestry Cross Cables!*

20th

Leeds fans go on rampage at Odsal Stadium, temporary home of Bradford City.... Nottingham Forest stay top after another six-goal romp, this time at Stamford Bridge where they beat Chelsea 6-2. Garry Birtles and David Webb each score hat-tricks.... Liverpool show their vulnerability again, losing 2-1 at Southampton.... Oldham remain top of the Second Division despite losing by the odd goal in nine at Huddersfield.... Celtic put five past Hibernian, while Dundee United remain top after putting five past Hamilton.

21st

Another defeat for Manchester United, this time they go down 3-1 at Everton who stay second to Forest.

22nd

After adhering to their 'home fans only' policy, Luton Town are expelled from the Littlewoods Cup, giving Cardiff City a bye to the 3rd round. ... Bristol Rovers sack reserve-team coach and manager Harold Jarman for the third time in 14 years! ... Billy McNeill leaves Manchester City and takes charge of Aston Villa.

SAINT: *Billy beware!*

23rd

Steve McMahon scores four goals, and misses a penalty, for Liverpool in 10-0 win over Fulham in Littlewoods Cup, equalling the competition's record win.... Renowned Cup fighters York beat Chelsea 1-0 and Fourth Division Preston hold West Ham to a 1-1 draw at Deepdale in front of 13,000 fans.... Manchester City cannot beat their Fourth Division opponents, Southend, drawing 0-0 at Roots Hall.... Watford held

1-1 at home by Rochdale.... In the Skol Cup, Celtic reach the Final after beating Motherwell 5-4 on penalties, after 120 minutes' play ended in a 2-2 draw.

GREAVSIE: *Saint says: 'We were robbed' – mind you he's biased*

24th
More Littlewoods Cup action: Manchester United struggle to beat Port Vale 2-0.... Holders Oxford have no such problems against Gillingham. John Aldridge scores four goals in a 6-0 win.... Billy McNeill sees his new team draw 1-1 at Reading, while Howard Kendall's team continues its winning ways with a 4-0 home win over Newport County.... League leaders Nottingham Forest held to a goalless draw at Brighton.... Happier times for Graeme Souness and Rangers: they beat Dundee United 2-1 to reach the Skol Cup Final.

27th
Aston Villa offer their new manager some cheer after a spirited 3-3 draw at Anfield.... Forest pull two points clear after a 1-0 home win over Arsenal. Nigel Clough scores after three minutes. Charlie Nicholas is carried off and, after Forest fans cheer, Brian Clough says angrily: 'I don't want those kind of people in the City Ground.'... Norwich move into second place after beating Newcastle 2-0 and Everton lose ground, going down 2-0 to two Clive Allen goals at Spurs.... Coventry are another surprise package, going fourth after beating Watford 1-0.... Wimbledon continue their slide down the table, drawing at home with Southampton.

SAINT: *Cloughie's no clown*

28th
Manchester United level on points with Aston Villa at the foot of the table after another home defeat, this time by Chelsea.

30th
Liverpool beat Everton 4-1 at Goodison to take Screensport Super Cup 7-2 on aggregate. Three goals from Ian Rush.... Middlesbrough, so near to extinction not so long ago, extend their unbeaten run to 11 matches in the Third Division, and create a club record for the best start-of-the-season run.... Northampton maintain their grip at the top of Division Four with a win at Halifax where there are nearly as many goals as fans! Northampton win 6-3; the fans total 1,034!

GREAVSIE: *Some late news: A break-in by fans at Northampton – the team wins!*

October

1st
Jimmy Frizzell, Billy McNeill's assistant at Manchester City, promoted to manager as McNeill's successor.... Mo Johnston scores both Celtic's goals in the 2-0 win over Shamrock Rovers in the European Cup, as they go through 3-0 on aggregate.... Aberdeen out of the Cup Winners' Cup, losing 4-2 on aggregate to Sion of Switzerland, but Wrexham have no problem beating their Maltese opponents Zurrieq, winning 7-0 on aggregate.... After beating Dukla

Prague 3–2 in the 1st leg of their UEFA Cup tie, Hearts lose the 2nd leg 1–0 and go out on the away goals rule.... Rangers uphold Scottish pride by going through 4–2 on aggregate against Tampere, despite losing the 2nd leg 2–0.

2nd

The Football League complete negotiations with *Today* newspaper, who announce a £4 million sponsorship deal with the League over two, possibly three years.

SAINT: *Announcer: 'It was announced yesterday Bryan Robson is unfit for tomorrow's Today League match'*

3rd

Mark Falco joins Watford from Spurs in a £350,000 deal.... Spurs then pay £600,000 for Belgian international striker Nico Claesen.... Manchester United beat off several other clubs for the signature of highly rated 21-year-old midfielder Liam O'Brien from Shamrock Rovers.

4th

As the Liverpool revival begins, the Wimbledon slide continues ... Wimbledon 1 Liverpool 3. The defending champions move into third place behind Forest, who draw 1–1 at home to Manchester United, and Norwich, who beat QPR 1–0.... Everton rocked by a Steve Williams goal which gives Arsenal a 1–0 win at Goodison.... Villa lift themselves off the bottom with a 1–0 win at Coventry.... The only unbeaten teams in the Football League are Portsmouth and Plymouth in the Second Division, Middlesbrough, top of the Third, and Cambridge and Exeter in the Fourth. Exeter's statistics: won two, drawn seven! ...

Dundee United and Celtic both win in Scotland while Rangers draw 1–1 with Hearts in front of a full house at Tynecastle.

6th

The FA re-impose the all-ticket ban on travelling Leeds United fans.... Brian Little sacked by Wolves after seven weeks as manager.... Sheffield Wednesday, without six regular first-teamers, still manage to beat Stockport County 7–0 at Maine Road in the Littlewoods Cup.

7th

Peter Barnes, playing only his second game in 11 months, plays a vital role in Manchester United's 5–2 defeat of Port Vale in 2nd leg of Littlewoods Cup.... Preston's hopes dashed by 4–1 defeat at West Ham, for whom Tony Cottee scores a hat-trick.... Liverpool score *ONLY* three in 2nd leg at Fulham, winning 3–2, but 13–2 on aggregate.... Everton score five at Newport, Wilkinson scores three.... Rochdale put up a brave fight losing 2–1 at home to Watford, but Wimbledon dumped out by Cambridge on the away goals rule.... Graham Turner, recently sacked by Aston Villa, appointed manager of Wolves.

GREAVSIE: *Wag of the Season: the Fulham programme editor. He writes: If teams are level at the end of 90 minutes, extra time will be played (Fulham 10 goals down)*

8th

Bradford City lose 1–0 at Newcastle but win through their Littlewoods Cup tie 2–1 on aggregate.... Chelsea put paid to York's giant-killing hopes with a 3–0 win and Villa beat Reading 4-1 to gain a 5-2 aggregate win.... Manchester City only just beat Southend 2-1 and Spurs win a 5-3 thriller against Barnsley, and go through 8-5 on aggregate.... Bobby Moore admitted to the University College Hospital suffering from a suspected heart complaint.... The FA back Luton's plan to ban away supporters, and will therefore allow them to compete in the FA Cup.

9th
Stoke boss Mick Mills signs former Ipswich colleague Brian Talbot from Watford for £25,000.

11th
Having won at Anfield two seasons ago for the first time since 1912, Spurs firmly lay the bogey with another victory at Anfield thanks to a Clive Allen goal, the only one of the game.... Forest knocked off top after losing 3-1 at Leicester.... Norwich the new leaders after goalless draw at Luton.... Spurs move third and West Ham fourth after beating Chelsea 5-3. Stewart scores a penalty and Cottee notches two goals in the last 10 minutes to set up the victory.... Manchester United ease their problems with a 3-1 home win over Sheffield Wednesday, but stay in 20th place.... Manchester City, on the other hand, go bottom after losing to fellow strugglers Newcastle.... Portsmouth beat Birmingham 2-0 to become the new leaders in the Second Division.... Despite losing at home to Blackpool, Middlesbrough stay top of the Third Division and Northampton establish a four-point gap at the top of Division Four.

SAINT: *Cobblers to the rest*

14th
Oxford United and Northern Ireland striker Billy Hamilton's career ends after a series of knee operations are unsuccessful.

15th
Gary Lineker scores two and Chris Waddle one as England beat Northern Ireland 3-0 at Wembley in the European Championship. Crowd only 35,000.... The Republic of Ireland and Scotland draw 0-0 in Dublin.

GREAVSIE: *High-scoring Scots strike again*

16th
Six weeks after joining Manchester City Robert Hopkins is off, to West Brom, as part of the deal that takes Imre Varadi to Maine Road. City also sell Trevor Christie to Walsall for £30,000.... Popular Everton goalkeeper of the 1930s, Ted Sagar, dies at the age of 76.... Watford bring back Steve Sims to Vicarage Road, two years after selling him to Notts County.

17th
Oldham return to the top of the Second Division following a 2-1 win over Millwall.... Northampton increase their lead at the top of Division Four with a 3-2 win at Cambridge.

18th
Norwich lose the First Division leadership after drawing 1-1 at home to fellow challengers West Ham.... Nottingham Forest return to the top after 1-0 home win over QPR, but the Merseyside giants show they cannot be ignored: Liverpool beat Oxford 4-0 while Everton win 2-0 at Southampton.... Manchester United get three valuable points thanks to a Frank Sta-

pleton goal that beats Luton.... Portsmouth lose their first match of the season, going down 3–1 at Leeds.... Plymouth also lose their unbeaten record, 4–2 at home to Sunderland.... Exeter remain the only unbeaten team in the League.... In Scotland, Celtic are new leaders but Rangers are only three points behind and looking good after a poor start to the season – they score five at Falkirk.

19th
Coventry beat Wimbledon 1–0 and the Londoners are criticized for their style of play – Coventry caught offside 22 times!

20th
Police called to a meeting of the Charlton Athletic Supporters' Club as hundreds of fans try to get into an already packed hall for a meeting aimed at getting the club to return to the Valley.... It is announced that several League clubs, angered at the FA's decision to back Luton Town, have been meeting secretly to discuss the possibility of running their own knockout competition.

SAINT: *Sponsored by British Rail and called 'The Awayday Cup'*

21st
A second half hat-trick by Mick Quinn in the 3–1 win over Derby sees Portsmouth back at the top of the Second Division.... Plymouth also return to winning ways, beating Ipswich 2–0.... Middlesbrough lose to Notts County in the Third Division but remain top on goal difference from Bournemouth who move into second place after beating Doncaster 3–2.... Fulham's lowest-ever gate at Craven Cottage, 2,361, sees them come back from 2–0 down to draw 2–2

with Bristol Rovers.... The Millwall–West Brom Full Members' Cup match watched by only 967.

22nd
Mo Johnston scores for Celtic who are held at home by Dynamo Kiev in the European Cup.... Butragueno scores the only goal of the game to give Real Madrid a slender lead over Juventus.... Wrexham draw 0–0 away to Real Zaragoza in the Cup Winners' Cup.... Dundee United build up a 1st leg lead of 3–0 over Universitatae Craiova.... In the League, Northampton continue their run in Division Four beating Burnley 4–2, their 29th goal in 11 matches.... Exeter remain unbeaten after beating Hartlepool 2–0.

23rd
Rangers concede the first goal at home to Boavista in the UEFA Cup but win 2–1. Graeme Souness has a recurrence of a calf injury that rules him out of the forthcoming Skol Cup Final.... Newcastle pay Bradford City £250,000 for their captain and centre half Peter Jackson.... Oldham pay Leeds £80,000 for Scottish Under-21 striker Tommy Wright, and Manchester City complete their third deal in a week when they sign Tony Grealish from West Brom for £20,000.

25th
Forest and Norwich both lose (to Oxford and Wimbledon) but stay first and second.... Everton go third after 3–2 home win over Watford but Liverpool's challenge knocked when they lose 4–1 at Luton. Mike Newell scores a hat-trick.... Arsenal join leaders following 3–1 win over Chelsea.... Portsmouth beat West Brom to stay top in Division Two and Bournemouth become

the new leaders in Division Three after beating Wigan 3–1 while Middlesbrough are held at Bristol City.... Exeter remain unbeaten in Division Four and Northampton increase lead to seven points.

26th
The 109th Manchester derby results in a 1–1 draw at Maine Road, with Mick McCarthy and Stapleton scoring the goals.... Rangers beat Celtic 2–1 to win the Skol Cup in front of 74,219 at Hampden Park.

GREAVSIE: *Silver for Souness, but shouldn't it be England 2 Celtic 1?*

27th
Northampton go 10 points clear at the top of Division Four after winning 3–0 at Stockport.

28th
Littlewoods Cup 3rd round: Arsenal easily dispose of Manchester City 3–1, and Everton have no problems with Sheffield Wednesday, winning 4–0.... But shocks for Ipswich who lose 1–0 at Cambridge and Chelsea who go down 2–1 at Cardiff.

29th
A Steve McMahon hat-trick sees Liverpool ease into the 4th round of the Littlewoods Cup at the expense of Leicester City. Liverpool win 4–1.... Manchester United and Southampton draw 0–0.... Watford lose 3–2 at home to West Ham and League leaders Forest are held 2–2 at Crystal Palace.... Second Division leaders Portsmouth knocked out by Bradford City, but no such problems for Spurs: they beat Birmingham 5–0 with Clive Allen bagging two more goals.... North of the border Celtic put six past Clydebank, while the top match, between Dundee United and Rangers, fails to produce a goal.... St Mirren captain Billy Abercromby sent off three times in the game against Motherwell. He protests so much he is shown the red card three times and receives five penalty points for each offence!

SAINT: *Maybe the lad was colour blind!*

November

1st
Norwich's title ambitions brought down to earth at Anfield where Liverpool win 6–2. Paul Walsh scores a hat-trick.... Forest stay top following 3–2 home win over Sheffield Wednesday.... Everton lose 1–0 at West Ham and Arsenal's 2–0 win at Charlton takes them second.... Wimbledon win 2–1 at Spurs.... Oldham and Portsmouth play out a goalless draw in the top-of-the-table game in Division Two, but Pompey stay top by one point.... Middlesbrough beat Bournemouth 4–0 in the top game in Division Three and in Division Four Northampton are eight points clear of Swansea.... Exeter lose their first match 2–1 at Preston.... Celtic and Rangers draw 1–1 in a bad-tempered match in Scotland, and Dundee United's 1–0 win at St Mirren puts them level at the top with Celtic.

2nd

John Wile leaves Peterborough by mutual consent; former manager Noel Cantwell tipped as his likely replacement.

3rd

Following the boardroom coup at 92nd club Stockport County, which sees Dragan Lukic ousted, manager Jimmy Melia leaves the club.... Celtic arrive in Kiev for their European Cup tie with their own food ration – a precaution after the Chernobyl disaster.

GREAVSIE: *Chicken Kiev perhaps?*

4th

Southampton beat Manchester United 4–1 in their Littlewoods Cup replay with substitute Le Tissier scoring twice.... Aston Villa have a good 2–1 win over Second Division promotion candidates Derby County.... Rangers beat Boavista 1–0 to notch up a 3–1 aggregate win in the UEFA Cup.... Charlton have their lowest attendance in their 65-year history for the visit of Birmingham in the Full Members' Cup – a mere 821.... Gillingham become new leaders of Division Three after 2–1 win over Blackpool.

5th

In the top European Cup match, Juventus beat Real Madrid 1–0 but Real win 3–1 on penalties.... Celtic lose 3–1 to Kiev and go out 4–1, and Wrexham are out of the Cup Winners' Cup after drawing 2–2 with Real Zaragoza, losing on the away goals rule.... Dundee United, however, progress in the UEFA Cup, beating Craiova 3–1 on aggregate.... At home, Forest beat Palace 1–0 in their Littlewoods Cup replay, thanks to a Nigel Clough goal 11 minutes from time....

Tony Dorigo advised he is eligible for an English passport, and thus added to the England Under-21 squad for the forthcoming match with Yugoslavia.

6th

Ron Atkinson is sacked as Manchester United manager and replaced by Aberdeen boss Alex Ferguson.... Paul Goddard leaves West Ham for Newcastle in a £415,000 deal.

SAINT: *Bad luck Atko – good luck Fergie!*

8th

Liverpool win 3–1 at QPR and go top of the table as Forest lose to a Nick Pickering goal at Coventry.... Arsenal miss their chance to go top when held to a goalless draw at home by West Ham.... And it is bad news for Manchester United's new manager Alex Ferguson: his team loses 2–0 at Oxford.... Portsmouth stay top of the Second Division, Middlesbrough go back to the top of the Third and Northampton stretch their lead to 10 points in the Fourth.... Up north, Celtic open up a two-point gap after a 2–1 win at Hamilton and Dundee United's shock home defeat by their Dundee neighbours.... Rangers also lose ground, going down 1–0 at home to Motherwell.... Northwich Victoria, with only eight fit men, pull three lads out of the crowd for their GM Vauxhall Conference game against Maidstone – and manage a 1–1 draw!

10th

Walsall defender Ken Armstrong forced to quit the game, without kicking a ball for the club since his £125,000 transfer from Birmingham City.

11th

In an effort to fight off Aberdeen's approach for assistant manager Sandy Jardine, Hearts promote him to joint manager alongside Alex MacDonald.

12th

Gary Mabbutt and Viv Anderson score for England in 2-0 win over Yugoslavia in the European Championship. Goalkeeper Chris Woods makes his competitive international debut because of Peter Shilton's injury.... Northern Ireland draw 0-0 in Turkey and Scotland go top of group seven after beating Luxembourg 3-0 at Hampden – Kenny Dalglish wins his 102nd cap.

GREAVSIE: *What a splendid result, Saint!*

13th

Ron Atkinson turns down the chance to take charge at Peterborough.... Marco van Basten presented with the Adidas Golden Boot award as Europe's top club scorer in 1985-6.

SAINT: *Big Ron at Peterborough – doesn't quite ring!*

15th

Arsenal win impressively at Southampton by four goals to nil, and go top of the table.... Forest slip again, this time 4-2 at Luton who are only two points off the lead.... Everton halt their temporary slide with a win at Leicester, but Manchester United drop to 21st after drawing 0-0 at Norwich.... In Division Two Portsmouth lose at Shrewsbury while Oldham beat Leeds 2-0 at Elland Road in the top game to return to the top of the table.... Blackburn, rooted at the bottom of the division, send a letter to the directors, signed by all the players, saying the slump is their fault and not the manager's.... In the 1st round of the FA Cup Caernarfon Town beat Stockport County 1-0, Wolves are held by Chorley, Burnley lose 3-0 to Telford United, Swansea can only draw 1-1 at Wealdstone, and Doncaster draw 2-2 at Whitby.

16th

Liverpool miss their chance to return to the top of the table when held 1-1 at home by Sheffield Wednesday. Ian Rush scores his 13th goal of the season.

GREAVSIE: *Unlucky for some*

17th

John Blackley resigns as manager of Hibernian who lie third from bottom of the Scottish Premier Division.

18th

Littlewoods Cup holders Oxford go out 1-0 to a Tony Cottee penalty at West Ham.... Arsenal beat Charlton 2-0, Southampton scrape home against Villa, but Mark Dennis is sent off for the 10th time in his career.... Shrewsbury also book a place in the last eight with a 1-0 home win over Cardiff City.... In the FA Cup, Wolves are held to a home draw by non-leaguers Chorley, while Doncaster beat battlers Whitby by the odd goal in five.

19th

Everton book a place in the quarter-finals of the Littlewoods Cup with a fine 4-1 win at Norwich, but Nottingham Forest do even better, beating Bradford City 5-0 away from home.... Liverpool and Coventry draw 0-0 at Highfield Road.... In Scotland, Celtic, Rangers, Dundee United and the managerless Aberdeen all win.... At a meeting between the government and football officials at the Department of the Environment, Sports Minister Dick Tracey insists it is the Prime Minister's view that there should be a 100 per cent identity card system in operation in Britain.

SAINT: *Maggie's 'view' – surely he means 'demand'*

20th

Swansea's FA Cup replay with Wealdstone abandoned after 94 minutes shortly after the Swans go into a 2-1 extra-time lead.

21st

Leeds crash to a third successive defeat when they go down 2-1 to Birmingham at St Andrews.

22nd

Arsenal go two points clear of Forest after a 3-0 win over Manchester City. Quinn, Adams and Anderson keep the Gunners at the top of the table.... Forest keep up their challenge with a 3-2 win over Wimbledon, while West Ham drop a valuable home point against Aston Villa.... Newcastle win the bottom-of-the-table battle at Stamford Bridge 3-1. Newcastle are bottom and Chelsea next to bottom.... Manchester United jump five places after their 1-0 win over QPR at Old Trafford.... Oldham stay top of the Second Division after beating Crystal Palace 1-0, but Portsmouth breathe down their necks after a 2-1 win over Grimsby. Plymouth and Derby also emerging as promotion candidates, just two points behind Pompey.... In the Third Division Middlesbrough, Gillingham and Bournemouth set the pace, with two points

separating the three of them – all three win.... Rangers' title hopes take a dent when they lose 1-0 at Aberdeen and Celtic increase their lead over Dundee United to four points, with a game in hand, after their 4-2 win over Falkirk. Hearts stay third after beating Dundee 3-1.

23rd

Everton and Liverpool draw the 135th Merseyside derby without a goal being scored. The crowd of 48,247 is the highest at an English League ground all season, despite the fact that the game is televised live.

GREAVSIE: *That must have pleased Clough and company*

24th

In the FA Cup replays Swansea eventually put paid to Wealdstone's brave efforts, winning 4-1, but three players are sent off.... Wolves lose 3-0 to Multipart Leaguers Chorley to slump to a new low.

26th

Mixed fortunes for the two Scottish clubs in the UEFA Cup.... Dundee United beat Hajduk Split 2-0 at home in their 1st leg tie but Rangers are held 1-1 by Borussia Moenchengladbach.... Spurs beat Cambridge in the Littlewoods Cup and Liverpool beat Coventry 3-1, all three goals coming from Molby penalties.

28th

Northampton maintain their run in the Fourth Division with a 5-0 win at Crewe. Richard Hill takes his tally for the season to 18 with a hat-trick.

29th

Arsenal's 4-0 win at Aston Villa makes sure they stay at the top of the table.... Forest within two points of them, coming from 2–1 down to win 3–2 at Spurs, despite Clive Allen knocking in two more goals.... Liverpool beat Coventry for the second time in a week to go third and Everton fill fourth place after their 3–1 win at Manchester City. Paul Power scored against his old club.... United, on the other hand, are still struggling to get away from the danger zone. Wimbledon beat them 1–0 and the scorer, Vince Jones, was three weeks earlier playing for Wealdstone in the GM Vauxhall Conference! ... The top Second Division game sees Plymouth beat Oldham 3–2, but the Lancastrians stay top just one point ahead of Argyle and Portsmouth, who draw at Millwall.... No change at the top of the Third Division,

although Middlesbrough and Gillingham lose, and Bournemouth do not play.... Celtic give a lacklustre performance in beating St Mirren 1–0, but their lead is extended to seven points as Falkirk win only their third game of the season, beating Dundee United 2–1. Hearts also lose, 3–0 at Rangers, to make Celtic favourites for the title.

30th
Newcastle move off the bottom of the table with an excellent 4–0 win over West Ham in one of the best live games seen on television.

SAINT: *Ha'way the Lads!*

December

1st
Ex-Ipswich Town and England defender Kevin Beattie becomes player–coach of Norwegian Third Division club Kongsverg.... Saints' 'Sinner' Mark Dennis strikes a charity deal with the PFA – if he's sent off again he'll pay £500 to charity; if not, the PFA will cough up!

GREAVSIE: *Get the sock out from under the bed, Mark*

2nd
Despite pleas from the Anfield fans, plus an offer to pay an extra 25p at the turnstiles each week to keep him, Ian Rush is definitely off to Juventus at the end of the season.... Bournemouth's largest crowd of the season, more than 7,000 watch them lose the top-of-the-table battle with Gillingham, who win 2–0.... In the Fourth

Division, Northampton score four more goals, past Exeter, to consolidate their position at the top of the table.... Ipswich beat Aston Villa 1–0 in the 3rd round of the Full Members' Cup and at Torquay, a mere 601 turn out for the Freight Rover Trophy match with Swansea ... had they known it was going to be 0–0 the crowd would have been even less!

3rd
A capacity 26,000 crowd at Tynecastle sees Hearts beat Celtic 1–0 and thus end the leaders' run of 16 matches without defeat. A Neil Berry header in the 33rd minute is good enough to give the home team victory.... In the Full Members' Cup Graeme Sharp scores a 39-minute hat-trick as Everton beat Newcastle 5–2.... And in front of 25,000 fans the highlight of Pat Jennings' testimonial in Belfast is a George Best goal

in the 3–3 draw between a British XI and a European XI.... Steve Perryman goes to Buckingham Palace during the day to collect his MBE. At night he helps his club Brentford to a 0–0 draw at Bristol Rovers in the FA Cup.

SAINT: *Well done Stevie, MBE*

4th

Brian Clough aims criticism at Mrs Thatcher and the Minister for Sport over plans to introduce identity cards.... Jan Molby signs a new four-year contract to stay at Liverpool until 1990.... Reading captain to sue Oldham's Ron Futcher after receiving a broken jaw in three places following an incident during their match at Elm Park on 25 October.

5th

Alex Miller, the former Rangers player, leaves St Mirren to take charge at Hibernian.... Rochdale dismiss manager Vic Halom, who has been at Spotland for two seasons.... Southend and Northampton, two high-fliers in the Fourth Division, fight a thrilling 4–4 draw in the 2nd round of the FA Cup at Roots Hall.

6th

In the Cup, Bath City score a last-minute equalizer in the local derby at Bristol City, while Caernarfon Town miss a last-minute goal that would have given them a 1–0 win over York.... Chorley are up to their antics again: this time they hold their illustrious neighbours, Preston, to a goalless draw in front of a 15,000 crowd at Blackburn's Ewood Park ground.... In the battle between the non-league giants, Telford beat Altrincham 1–0.... In the League,

Arsenal maintain their two-point lead with a 3–1 win over QPR, but Forest will not let them get away. They beat Manchester City, who stay bottom, 2–0.... Everton jump over Liverpool into third place after their 4–0 home win against Norwich while their neighbours lose 2–0 at Watford.... Wimbledon's 4–0 win at Stamford Bridge pulls them clear of the relegation zone and into a mid-table position.... Ron Atkinson turns down the chance to manage Rochdale until the end of the season.... Plymouth lose 1–0 at Stoke and Plymouth's defeat means Northampton is the only one of the League's 92 clubs to have scored in every game this season.... A boring day in the Scottish Premier Division – the six matches produce a total of three goals and Celtic scored two in their 2–0 win over Dundee.... Falkirk beat Motherwell 1–0 to score the other.

GREAVSIE: *The disease is spreading to club football, Saint!*

7th

Maidstone United are the only non-League side to knock out League opposition in the Cup over the weekend when they beat Cambridge United 1–0.... Notts County lose at home by the same score to Third Division promotion hopefuls Middlesbrough.... In the League, Manchester United and Spurs shared the honours in a six-goal thriller at Old Trafford.

9th

Nottingham Forest sign Norwegian international Ossie Osvold from champions Lillestrom. He will join Forest in the New Year.... Caernarfon win themselves a home FA Cup 3rd round tie against Barnsley after beating York City 2–1 at Bootham

Crescent.... No such fantasy for Bath: they lose 3-0 to Bristol City and Chorley bid farewell to this season's competition, losing 5-0 at Preston, but not until they receive another share of a large gate, nearly 16,500.... In Dubai, Liverpool and Celtic play an exhibition match. Liverpool win a penalty shoot-out 4-3 after the game ends 1-1.

SAINT: *Couldn't they have met at Carlisle?*

10th
Davie Cooper and Stuart Munro are sent off for Rangers as they go out of the UEFA Cup after drawing 0-0 with Borussia Moenchengladbach, who win on the away goals rule.... Better fortune for Dundee United. 'Keeper Billy Thomson makes some magnificent saves at Hajduk Split in their goalless draw which assures them a place in the quarter-finals 2-0 on aggregate.... A crowd of just 7,200 see Cambridge beat Oxford 4-3 in the Varsity match at Wembley.... Northampton beat Southend 3-2 in their FA Cup replay and earn a trip to First Division Newcastle.

11th
FIFA announce that the profit from the 1986 World Cup is $42.5 million from a turnover of $85.7 million.

GREAVSIE: *More new blazers for the FA*

12th
Mark Dennis is in trouble again: this time his club Southampton ban him for seven days following a newspaper article in which he refers to a fight with Peter Shilton.

13th
Arsenal gain a point on Forest at the top of the First Division after drawing 1-1 at Norwich, while Brian Clough's team loses 3-2 at lowly Newcastle.... Everton fall three points behind Forest after losing on Luton's artificial pitch.... Manchester United and Aston Villa share six goals at Villa Park, while United's neighbours, City, beat West Ham and move off the bottom of the table, leaving Chelsea as new occupants of 22nd place.... With Oldham's game at Blackburn postponed, Portsmouth could take over at the top of Division Two, but instead lose 1-0 at Sheffield United. Four men are sent off (three from Portsmouth) for the first time in one game since the Crewe-Bradford game in 1955. A total of 13 are sent off on the day.... Middlesbrough are the only winners in the top three in the Third Division, but a new face enters the promotion race – Notts County go third after beating York 5-1.... Northampton are held 2-2 at home by Wrexham in the Fourth Division, but go 13 points clear as Swansea lose 4-0 at Lincoln.... It is back to scoring goals in the Scottish Premier Division.... Hearts put seven past Hamilton and Dundee score six against St Mirren in a nine-goal thriller.... Celtic drop a point at Motherwell and their lead over Dundee United is cut to five points.... In Tokyo, River Plate of Argentina beat Steaua Bucharest 1-0 to win the World Club Championship.

14th
Liverpool move back into third place by beating bottom club Chelsea 3-0.... And at Bradford there is an emotional return to Valley Parade for City who play an England XI in front of their new stand. City win 2-1 in front of a 15,000 crowd.

15th

Telford are told by local police that they cannot stage their home 3rd round FA Cup tie with Leeds at their Buck's Head ground because the police cannot cope. The matter is referred to the FA.

16th

The FA order Telford to play their FA Cup tie against Leeds at The Hawthorns, home of West Brom and scene of two major crowd disturbances involving Leeds 'fans' in the past four years.... Glenn Hoddle states he intends leaving Spurs at the end of the season to play on the continent.... Aldershot announce they are increasing the price of admission for their FA Cup tie with First Division Oxford by more than 300 per cent.

SAINT: *Rough justice for Telford*

17th

Former Stirling Albion manager Alex Smith is appointed manager of St Mirren.

18th

Mark Dennis is to be charged by the FA with bringing the game into disrepute following his newspaper article involving Peter Shilton.

20th

Nottingham Forest drop two more points, being held to a 0-0 draw by Southampton, and Arsenal's 3-0 home win over Luton increases their lead at the top of the table to five points.... Liverpool can only draw at Charlton while Everton complete the double over Wimbledon to share third place with Liverpool on 35 points, just one behind Forest.... Chelsea's misery continues with a 2-0 home defeat by Spurs. Clive Allen scores both Spurs goals.... Portsmouth go back to the top of the Second Division.... Celtic's lead is cut to four points in Scotland after they are held to a 1-1 draw by Aberdeen, maintaining the Dons' unbeaten record since Ian Porterfield took over as manager.... Rangers move into third place, just six points behind Celtic, after beating Hamilton.

21st

Manchester City ease their relegation worries with a 2-2 draw at Coventry and Sheffield Wednesday reap the rewards for switching their home match with Newcastle to Sunday. The crowd of 28,897 is the second highest of the season at Hillsborough, and their 2-0 win means they complete the double over United for the first time since 1956.... In the Second Division Oldham go back to the top after beating Bradford City at home.... Derby County move into third place after a 4-0 win over Grimsby and at the Victoria Ground Stoke's great revival continues with a resounding 7-2 win over Leeds United.... Middlesbrough displace Gillingham at the head of Division Three after winning 1-0 at Brentford.... In Division Four Northampton are at it again, beating eighth-placed Lincoln City by three goals to one.... Spurs agree to buy Steve Hodge from Aston Villa for £650,000, shortly after selling Graham Roberts to Glasgow Rangers, the fifth Anglo to join Graeme Souness' team since the summer.

GREAVSIE: *Are there any Scots left in Rangers' team, Saint?*

22nd

The on-off saga of Halifax Town's survival ends when they agree a deal with a property company that guarantees their survival until the end of the season – at least.

23rd

Mick Buxton, the longest-serving manager outside the First Division, is sacked by Huddersfield Town. He had been at the club since 1978. He is succeeded as longest serving outside the top flight by Gillingham's Keith Peacock.

26th

Arsenal can only draw at Leicester and Nottingham Forest lose 2-1 at Norwich.... Everton move second, four points behind the Gunners, after a power display that sees them win 4-0 at St James's Park, with Trevor Steven bagging two goals.... Liverpool are rocked by a Norman Whiteside goal giving United a 1-0 win at Anfield.... Clive Allen scores two more for Spurs in their 4-0 win over West Ham.... Oldham draw in the Second Division as the merry-go-round continues with Pompey going back to the top after a 3-2 win at Plymouth in front of 21,000 fans.... Middlesbrough win and Gillingham draw, which means both teams level on 41 points at the top of the Third Division.... Northampton go a staggering 17 points clear in the Fourth Division after their 4-0 rout of nearest challengers Southend. All other challengers can only draw.... A record crowd for the GM Vauxhall Conference of 4,130 sees Barnet beat Enfield 1-0.

SAINT: *An 'up' of 4,000 from your days at Barnet, Greavsie*

27th

Liverpool make amends for their defeat by United by winning 1-0 at Sheffield Wednesday, but a goal from Niall Quinn is enough to give Arsenal a win over Southampton and increase their lead to seven points. Liverpool go second above Everton and Forest, who do not play.... Manchester United, after their great display at Anfield, are brought back down to earth, losing 1-0 at home to one-time table-toppers Norwich. Bryan Robson is injured again and could be out for a month.... Portsmouth do not have a game in Division Two and are replaced as leaders by Derby County, who beat Barnsley 3-2.... Oldham lose at home to Leeds and Stoke City add to their seven-goal drubbing of the Elland Road team by scoring another five past Sheffield United and, in less than two months, have hauled themselves from relegation to promotion candidates.... Bournemouth are back in the promotion race in Division Three with their second holiday win, 3-2 over Fulham.... Middlesbrough drop a point at Mansfield, Gillingham lose at home to Swindon and Notts County move into second place, four points behind 'Boro, after winning 2-0 at Bury.... In Scotland, Celtic draw at Clydebank and drop their fifth point in five games, while Rangers beat Dundee United 2-0 and move ahead of them on goal difference ... just five points behind their Glasgow rivals.

28th

Everton are back in second place after a 5-1 beating of Leicester, a defeat which pushes City to the bottom of the table on goal difference from Newcastle.... Nottingham Forest drop two valuable home points against Luton in a 2-2 draw and at Selhurst Park Charlton win the bottom-of-the-table battle against Manchester City by five goals to nil.... The Northampton goal machine rolls on, beating Cardiff 4-1 in front of 11,138 fans.

29th

All change again in Division Two as Portsmouth beat Shrewsbury 3–0 and go top once more.

30th

Bobby Saxton becomes the second Christmas managerial sacking when Blackburn dismiss him. He succeeded Howard Kendall as manager at Ewood Park in May 1981.... Torquay United install individual showers in the dressing rooms as the players refuse to use a communal bath for fear of catching AIDS.

GREAVSIE: *And to think of whom I shared a bath with at Spurs!*

January

1st

Arsenal, Portsmouth, Middlesbrough, Northampton, Celtic, Dunfermline and Raith top the tables on New Year's Day.... Rangers beat Celtic 2–0.... Kevin Moran swallows his tongue at Newcastle and is saved by physio Jim McGregor.

3rd

Leicester win 6–1 against Sheffield Wednesday to move off bottom of the First Division.... Celtic thrash the Accies 8–3.... Liam O'Brien (Manchester United) sent off after 104 seconds at Southampton.... Ken Bates gives supporters his tickets for the game at Luton.

SAINT: *Out of order, Mr Bates*

4th

The 100th Arsenal *v* Spurs match is won 2–1 by the Gunners at White Hart Lane.

5th

Alan Mullery is sacked by Brighton, the fourth sacking in 14 days in the bottom half of Division Two.... John Aldridge travels to Liverpool to sign for the League champions.

6th

Stewart Robson goes to West Ham for £700,000.... Aldridge to stay at Oxford for a month.

GREAVSIE: *Robert Maxwell strikes again*

10th

FA Cup 3rd round ... Walsall beat Charlton 1–0 ... Palace beat Forest 1–0 on the same pitch a day later.... Caernarfon draw 0–0 with Barnsley.... Norman Whiteside wins the Manchester derby for United.... Aldershot beat Oxford 3–0 watched by only 1,996 fans: cheapest ticket £9!

SAINT: *Nice to see a club giving their fans a break!*

11th

Telford forced to play at West Brom and lose 2–1 to Leeds.... Palace beat Forest.

14th

Luton fail to turn up at Anfield though pitch is in perfect condition. The troubles start ... snow hits the country.

16th

Alan Brazil forced to retire from the game with back trouble. QPR cancel his contract.

21st

Arsenal beat Forest 2–0 and Liverpool win at Goodison 1–0 to go into semi-finals of Littlewoods Cup…. Newcastle beat Northampton 2–1 in FA Cup.

22nd

Liverpool buy Derek Statham after Jim Beglin is found to have broken his leg.

23rd

Statham's move is off after medical.

GREAVSIE: *Tragic – Derek is one of the best full backs in Britain*

24th

Chris Woods of Rangers equals British record with 12th clean sheet…. David Rocastle sent off in turbulent match at Old Trafford…. Frank McLintock leaves Brentford.

27th

Southampton beat Shrewsbury; Spurs draw with West Ham in the other of the Littlewoods Cup quarter-finals.

28th

Liverpool lose 3–0 on the Luton plastic in 3rd round, 2nd replay…. Lawrie McMenemy takes £75,000 pay cut.

SAINT: *You've got to feel sorry for Big Lawrie*

29th

Keith Burkinshaw goes to Sporting Lisbon…. Mark Reid escapes with reprimand for felling ref Axcell on 3 January.

31st

Boring round of FA Cup, the 4th round has a shock when Wigan beat Norwich 1–0, Chester draw with Sheffield Wednesday, and Manchester United lose to Coventry…. The shock of the day comes in Scotland – Chris Woods sets British record of 1,196 minutes without conceding a goal but Hamilton Accies beat Rangers 1–0 in the Cup at Ibrox. Policeman Adrian Sprott is the Accies hero…. Gary Lineker scores hat-trick against Real Madrid.

GREAVSIE: *In the secret diary of Adrian Sprott: Accies 1 The English 0. Well done my lads!*

February

1st

Luther Blissett's goal knocks Chelsea out of the Cup.

2nd

Clive Allen's hat-trick sinks West Ham 5–0 in Littlewoods Cup replay…. Clough transfer lists Franz Carr and blames Carr's father…. Luton agree to compensate Liverpool for failing to turn up on 14 January.

SAINT: *How do you pay for 20,000 pies?*

4th

QPR win plastic Cup tie 2–1 in replay against Luton…. Ian Knight (Sheffield Wednesday) breaks leg in tackle from Bennett of Chester – Wednesday win 3–1…. Dalglish blasts Luton, could be in trouble.

8th

Spurs win TV match at Arsenal 1-0 in Littlewoods Cup semi-final.

9th

Tony Adams called up by England for match against Spain.

11th

Paul Walsh sent off in flare-up at the Dell: 0-0 in first Littlewoods Cup semi-final.... Speedie doesn't go to Villa.

GREAVSIE: *Who can blame him?*

14th

Peter Reid back for Everton after World Cup injury.... Rush gets another three against Leicester.

18th

Wimbledon reveal plans to go to Selhurst Park; start of the London merger talks.... Lineker gets all four in Spain.... Scots lose 1-0 in European Championship to Eire at Hampden.... Northern Ireland draw 1-1 in Israel and Wales hold Russia 0-0 in Swansea.

SAINT: *I'll say it before you Greavsie: we were murder*

21st

Gary Bailey returns after a year out.... in the Cup Leeds beat QPR 2-1 and Wigan beat Hull 3-0. Leeds and Wigan drawn against each other in next round.... Walsall and Watford 1-1.

22nd

Wimbledon beat Everton 3-1 in 5th round of FA Cup.

23rd

Day 1 of the Fulham saga.... Fulham Park Rangers at Loftus Road, whilst Craven Cottage goes to Marler Estates.... Nigel Spackman signs for Liverpool for £400,000.

24th

Watford and Walsall draw 4-4 at Walsall in Cup replay.

25th

Sheffield Wednesday win in the Cup 2-0 at Upton Park.... Liverpool beat Southampton 3-0 in Littlewoods Cup to go to Wembley.... Merger mania.... Wigan told to play Leeds in the Cup on a Sunday.

GREAVSIE: *Why do Leeds get all the breaks?*

26th

Souness shows interest in Ray Houghton, a Catholic....

28th

Fulham draw 2-2 with Walsall, QPR beat Manchester City 1-0, Newcastle lose at Wimbledon 3-1 - all three grounds stage merger protests.

March

1st

Arsenal win at Spurs 2-1 and save Littlewoods Cup semi-final – 2-2 on aggregate.... John Aldridge scores winner against Southampton on home debut.

2nd

Liam Brady is set for Upton Park.... Watford win 1-0 at Walsall at last.... David Webb leaves Southend, who are third!

4th

Spurs lose 2-1 at home again to Arsenal, who go to Wembley to meet Liverpool in the Littlewoods Cup Final.... Dundee United beat Barcelona 1-0 in UEFA quarter-finals 1st leg.

5th

League offer Maradona £350 per minute to play in their centenary match.... Spurs still persist with Maradona interest.... Palace crowd rejects merger with Wimbledon.... Wayne Clarke goes to Everton.... Fulham saved – by Jimmy Hill!

SAINT: *Well done 'the beard'*

7th

Everton lose to Watford in TV game – Liverpool go top.

10th

Arsenal lose vital game at home to Liverpool – Rush goal.... UEFA ban stays.

12th

Sports Minister Dick Tracey supports ban on English fans abroad.... Oxford sign Dean Saunders from Brighton for £60,000.

13th

Diego Maradona extends his contract with Napoli until 1993.... Mark Kelly, the 17-year-old Portsmouth winger, described by Alan Ball as the 'new George Best', opts to play for the Republic of Ireland ahead of England.... Burnley ease their relegation worries with a 1-0 win at Stockport County.

14th

Watford beat Arsenal 3-1 at Highbury in the 6th round of the FA Cup. Their goalscorers: Blissett (two) and Barnes.... Coventry enjoy a 3-1 win at Hillsborough thanks to two goals from Keith Houchen and one from Cyrille Regis.... In the League, Everton beat Southampton 3-0, while Liverpool remain six points clear at the top after a 3-1 win at Oxford.

15th

Wigan's Cup dreams end with a 2-0 home defeat by Leeds. The crowd of 12,250 is the lowest at this stage of the competition since the war, beating the previous lowest of 14,195 for Bradford City *v* Southampton in 1976.

16th

Don Howe agrees to help Southend in a coaching capacity until the end of the season.... FA Cup semi-final draw: Coventry *v* Leeds at Hillsborough; Watford *v* Spurs at Villa Park – Watford furious at having to travel up motorway for game against Spurs.

GREAVSIE: *And quite right too, Elton!*

17th

Sunderland deep in trouble following 3–0 defeat at Stoke.

18th

Dundee United win 2–1 at Barcelona and go through to UEFA Cup semi-final 3–1 on aggregate.... Neil Midgley appointed Cup Final referee, his first game at Wembley was the 1980 FA Vase in front of 13,000 people! ... Ian Rush scores his 200th and 201st goals for Liverpool in the 2–1 win at home to QPR to go nine points clear, but Everton have two games in hand.... Brazilian star Socrates announces his retirement in order to pursue career as a doctor.... Don Howe dismisses reports he is helping Southend!

SAINT: *Neil Midgley was once a promising footballer – until his eyesight failed*

19th

Blackpool sell striker Paul Stewart to Manchester City for £200,000, who immediately recoup the money by selling full back Clive Wilson to Chelsea.... West Ham buy Gary Strodder from Lincoln City for £100,000 as a replacement for Alvin Martin and Paul Hilton who are both injured.... It is revealed that Stoke City defender Chris Hemming has become the first professional footballer to be fitted with a heart pacemaker. The announcement is made after he comes through the 3–0 win over Sunderland without any problems.

GREAVSIE: *Amazing – I need one to lift my pipe these days*

20th

Celtic ban Mo Johnston for seven days following his appearance, and £500 fine, in court following an assault.... Frank Stapleton turns down a loan move to Manchester City.... Nottingham Forest sign Norwegian international midfielder Ossie Osvold for £90,000.... Barcelona drop Mark Hughes and bring back Steve Archibald.

21st

Everton close gap at top with narrow 2–1 win over Charlton at Goodison. Trevor Steven (pen.) and Gary Stevens, seven minutes from time, clinch victory.... Southampton put Villa deeper in trouble with a 5–0 win at the Dell.... Ten players sent off during the weekend matches.

22nd

Spurs beat Liverpool 1–0 at White Hart Lane thanks to 39th minute goal from Waddle, and Nottingham Forest jump two places to fourth following a hard-fought 2–1 win over Leicester City.

23rd

Alex Ferguson trying to get Mark Hughes back from Barcelona.... Scotland drop Mo Johnston.... Bobby Robson names an unchanged squad for only the third time in five years, for the European Championship match against Northern Ireland.

24th

Richard Hill, Northampton's top scorer, signs for Watford for £235,000.... Everton centre forward Paul Wilkinson joins Nottingham Forest for £275,000.... Brentford pay a club record £60,000 for Crewe striker Gary Blissett.... Darlington part company with manager Cyril Knowles and coach John Craggs: 24-year-old club captain

Paul Ward is appointed caretaker player-manager.... Portsmouth reach an out-of-court settlement with former manager Bobby Campbell, who has been suing for £80,000.

SAINT: *That'll teach 'em!*

25th

Swansea's promotion hopes dashed when the Football League deduct three points from them for cancelling their fixture with Rochdale on 3 March. They have 14 days in which to appeal.... The FA fine John Bond for a newspaper attack on Bobby Robson .... Sammy McIlroy scores his first goal for his new club, Bury, in the 1–0 win at Chester.... Barcelona beat Osasuna 4–2 to go ahead of Real Madrid in the Spanish League. Lineker scores two, Archibald one .... At the bottom of the First Division, Newcastle and Villa both draw at home.

26th

Transfer-deadline day ... some of the important moves:

   Alan Smith, Leicester to Arsenal:
      £800,000
   Martin Foyle, Aldershot to Oxford:
      £140,000
   Tommy McQueen, Aberdeen to West
      Ham: £125,000
   Garth Crooks, West Brom to Charlton;
      £75,000

   Gerry Daly, Shrewsbury to Stoke City:
      £15,000
   Steve Lynex, Leicester to West Brom:
      £5,000
   Billy Bingham to quit Saudi club Al Nasr
      of Riyadh.

GREAVSIE: *I'll bet he came home with more than a tan*

28th

Liverpool lose 2–1 at home to Wimbledon, while Everton win at Highbury. Everton three points behind with a game in hand.... Manchester City bottom after 4–0 defeat at Leicester.... Mark Lawrenson out for rest of season after rupturing an Achilles' tendon.

29th

Colin Hendry scores only goal of the game to win the Full Members' Cup for Blackburn against Charlton in front of 40,000 fans at Wembley.

31st

Sunderland's troubles continue to pile up after 2–0 defeat at Birmingham.... Because of Peterborough's defeat at Torquay, Northampton become the first club to win promotion this season.... Andy Jones of Port Vale named in Welsh team to play Finland at Wrexham; two years ago he was playing non-League soccer!

April

1st

European Championships: England beat Northern Ireland 2–0 in Belfast (Robson and Waddle) ... Wales 4 (Rush, Hodges, Phillips, Jones) Finland 0 ... Belgium 4 (Spurs' Nico Claesen 3) Scotland 1 (McStay).

SAINT: *Mumble, mumble*

2nd

Norman Whiteside aggravates a groin strain against England and is out of United side for two–three weeks.... Arsenal sign a new shirt sponsorship deal with JVC, worth £500,000 over three years.

3rd

Former Welsh international Trevor Hockey collapses and dies after playing in a five-a-side tournament in his home-town of Keighley. He was only 43.... In the top-of-the-table Fourth Division battle, Preston beat Northampton 1–0 in front of a massive 16,456 crowd.

4th

Clive Allen takes his total goals for the season to 43. He scores all three in the 3–0 win over Norwich City.... Everton win 2–1 at Chelsea to go top of the table on goal difference, but still have a game in hand.... Villa and Manchester City play out a goalless draw at the bottom of the table, while Newcastle beat Leicester 2–0.... Derby go top of the Second Division with a 2–0 win at Ipswich, while Portsmouth lose at Bradford City.... Celtic beat Rangers 3–1 in top clash north of the border.

5th

Two Charlie Nicholas goals see Arsenal beat Liverpool 2–1 in Littlewoods Cup Final at Wembley, and that after Ian Rush scores first – the first time Liverpool have lost in the 144 matches in which Rush has scored.

6th

The Football League announce that red and yellow cards are to be re-introduced next season.... Rumours that Elton John is about to sell Watford for £3 million dismissed.

GREAVSIE: *Any truth in the rumour that someone wanted to rename the club: 'Queen of the South'?*

7th

Clive Allen scores only goal in Spurs' 1–0 win at Sheffield Wednesday, to take tally to 44 which either equals or beats Greaves' record ... there is some confusion over how many Greavsie scored! ... Jimmy Hill, chairman-designate of Fulham, assures manager Ray Lewington that his future with the club is secure. (Oops! there goes the kiss of death....)

8th

Dundee United held at home in UEFA Cup by Borussia Moenchengladbach.... West Ham beat Arsenal 3–1 and Newcastle beat Norwich 4–1 to get out of the bottom three for the first time since Christmas.... Derby consolidate their position at the top of the Second Division with a 2–0 win against Huddersfield, while Northampton suffer a rare defeat, at Hereford.... General Motors consider withdrawing their sponsorship of English football, worth £4 million.

9th

Steve Sherwood, Watford's 'keeper for the injured Tony Coton, dislocates a finger and could be out of FA Cup semi-final.... Jimmy Hill becomes chairman of Fulham, which has a new board.

10th

Brentford player–manager Steve Perryman decides to return to the side to play his 900th League and Cup game....

Colchester beat Burnley 1-0 to put the Lancastrians deeper in trouble.... The Coventry Youth team make it a good year for the city by beating Manchester City to reach the FA Youth Cup Final.

SAINT: *Sky Blues on their way*

11th

Everton move three points clear of Liverpool after a 4-0 win over West Ham while Liverpool lose 2-1 at Norwich.... Ian Rush scores as well ... they never win when he scores! ... Clive Allen definitely surpasses Greaves' record by scoring one goal in Spurs' 4-1 win over Watford in Cup semifinal. Watford 'keeper is Gary Plumley, son of the club's secretary, who is plucked out of obscurity to help out. He is to blame for two of the goals.

12th

Coventry beat Leeds 3-2 after extra time in thrilling FA Cup semi-final at Hillsborough to reach their first FA Cup Final. Goals from Michael Gynn, Keith Houchen and Dave Bennett assure them of their place.

13th

Leeds reward Billy Bremner with a new contract following FA Cup run.... Manchester United announce plans for identity card system for Stretford Road end and United Road paddock fans for next season .... Johnny King rejoins Tranmere as manager, the third man in charge at Prenton Park this season.... Four referees, due to retire at the end of the season, are asked to stay on beyond the normal retiring age – George Tyson, Neville Ashley, Colin Downey and John Martin.... David O'Leary recalled to Eire squad after absence of more than a year for match against Belgium on 29 April.

14th

Bryan Robson damages his right ankle in goalless draw against West Ham at Upton Park.... Arsenal lose 1-0 at home to Newcastle.... Bournemouth 11 points clear at the top of the Third Division after setting a club record of 25 wins in a season as they end Wigan's run of 17 home games without defeat.... Coventry turn down £18,000 from National Express to ride in one of their coaches down Wembley way – they decide to stick with their regular firm.

GREAVSIE: *Victory coaches?*

15th

Ray Clemence equals Pat Jennings' British first-class record of 1,097 appearances in the 1-1 draw at Maine Road.... Alex Ferguson fined £500 for being abusive to referee Ken Baker.... Lawrie McMenemy sacks assistant Lew Chatterley and much-travelled winger Terry Curran.... Mick Buxton appointed new manager of Scunthorpe.

16th

McMenemy leaves Sunderland; Bob Stokoe returns.... Mark Dennis reinstated by Southampton.... Brian Clough signs 20-year-old striker Billy Stubbs from Seaham Red Star and then says: 'I'm delighted for him, but I'm the world's worst judge of a striker. Remember, I paid £3 million for Peter Ward, Ian Wallace and Justin Fashanu.'

18th

Everton win 1-0 at Villa while Liverpool

beat Forest 3–0.... At the bottom of the League, Burnley win 2–0 at Rochdale in the relegation battle.... In Scotland, Rangers win 3–0 at Clydebank while Celtic are held 1–1 at home by Dundee United, for whom John Clark equalizes two minutes from time.

19th
Everton increase lead to six points, with a game in hand, after 3–0 home win over Newcastle – Wayne Clarke scores a hat-trick.... Liverpool lose 1–0 at Manchester United to a last-minute goal from Peter Davenport. Bruce Grobbelaar breaks an elbow and is out for the rest of the season.... Manchester City and Villa well adrift at the bottom after 2–1 and 3–0 defeats at Sheffield Wednesday and Charlton respectively.... Portsmouth lose at home to Plymouth in front of 17,000 fans.

21st
Peter Reid and Tony Cottee recalled to the England squad for the game against Northern Ireland on 29 April.

22nd
Dundee United win 2–0 in Borussia to beat Moenchengladbach 2–0 on aggregate in UEFA Cup semi-final.... Real Madrid beat Bayern Münich in European Cup, but lose 4–2 on aggregate, while FC Porto beat Dynamo Kiev 2–1 to win the other semi-final.... At home, Wimbledon's Brian Gayle is sent off in 2–2 draw with Spurs, but Dave Bassett maintains Nico Claesen has made a 'meal' of the incident.

23rd
Gary Bailey forced to retire at the age of 28 with a crippling knee injury.... Swansea successfully appeal against their three point-deduction imposed by the League.

24th
Peter Shilton out of England team to meet Turkey because of a stomach strain.... Southampton's Mark Dennis joins QPR for £50,000.... A crowd of 10,139 watch Southend's top-of-the-table clash with Wolves – the home side win 1–0 thanks to a Ling goal.

25th
On the international front, Joey Jones called out of international retirement and into the Welsh squad for the game with Czechoslovakia, while Leicester's captain Ian Wilson gains his first Scottish call-up at the age of 29.... Clydebank striker Stuart Gordon in intensive care with fractured skull following accidental clash of heads in game against Dundee.... Manchester City beat Arsenal 3–0, but in the top-of-the-table clash Liverpool beat Everton 3–1 with Ian Rush scoring two goals and equalling Dixie Dean's record of 19 goals in derby matches.

SAINT: *What a way to go!*

28th
Bradford City beat Sunderland 3–2, at Roker, for the second time in 10 days.... Oldham strengthen their promotion hopes with an excellent 3–0 win at Stoke City.... In the Third Division, Middlesbrough beat Gillingham 3–0, while Swindon win the division's top battle by beating Notts County 3–2 at Meadow Lane.... In Division Four, Preston beat Tranmere 2–0 in front of their fifth 10,000-plus crowd of the season .... Burnley lose at Scunthorpe while Torquay push the Turf Moor team deeper into trouble by beating Cardiff 1–0.

29th

European Championship: Turkey 0 England 0; Wales 1 (Rush) Czechoslovakia 1; Northern Ireland 1 (Clarke) Yugoslavia 2; Eire 0 Belgium 0.... Scarborough win the GM Vauxhall Conference and a place in the League after Barnet lose at home to Stafford Rangers.... West Brom beat Portsmouth 1-0 and delay Pompey's guaranteed return to the First Division.... Halifax and Colchester draw 0-0 at the Shay in front of the League's lowest crowd of the season,

911.... Burnley go bottom of the League after Rochdale's 2-0 win over Swansea.

GREAVSIE: *You know it's not the right time of the year for turkey, Saint!*

30th

Coventry win 3-2 at Watford in a re-arranged fixture designed to leave them clear of matches in Cup Final week.... Southend's promotion hopes in Division Four take a knock as they lose 4-0 at Wrexham.

May

2nd

Nick Pickering scores the only goal of the game to give Coventry a 1-0 win over Liverpool, virtually handing the title to Everton, even though Everton are held to a goalless draw by Manchester City. Everton need one win from their last three games to win the title.... Derby edge nearer the Second Division title with a 2-1 home win over Leeds, but Portsmouth are still with them, three points behind.... Bournemouth clinch promotion from Division Three while Carlisle, Newport and Darlington all assure themselves of Fourth Division football.... Preston's goalless draw with Peterborough gives Northampton the Fourth Division title they looked like winning six months ago.... Rangers draw at Aberdeen, but Graeme Souness is sent off again. Celtic's home defeat by Falkirk means Rangers are the new champions.

SAINT: *Two out of three for Terry and Co. - and haven't they learned the highland fling quickly?*

4th

Pat Van Den Hauwe scores a first-minute goal, which is enough for Everton to beat Norwich at Carrow Road and clinch the title.... Ian Rush scores the only goal against Watford at Anfield on his farewell appearance, in front of 40,000 fervent fans.... At the bottom of the table Leicester lose two valuable points at home to Cup finalists Coventry.... But fellow Midlanders Aston Villa definitely relegated after losing 2-1 at home to Sheffield Wednesday.... Charlton ease their worries with a fine 3-0 win at Newcastle, and Manchester City claim all three points in a 1-0 home win over Nottingham Forest.... In the Second Division Derby lose at Reading, but Portsmouth fail to capitalize as they lose at Crystal Palace in front of an 18,000 crowd.... Brighton return to the Third Division after 10 years and in the Fourth Division, Wolves beat Exeter to improve their play-off chances, Rochdale beat Halifax 5-3 which means Burnley slump to the dreaded 92nd place after losing 1-0 at Crewe. Burnley file an objection to the Football League, saying the game was stopped three minutes early. 'Three minutes is a lifetime in football,' says manager Brian Miller.

GREAVSIE: *It's even longer in a Party Political Broadcast mate!*

5th
Oxford win 3-2 at Luton to guarantee themselves First Division football.... Oldham's slim chance of promotion from the Second Division disappears when they lose 2-0 at Shrewsbury, who ease themselves nearer safety.... Sunderland fall deeper in trouble after only drawing at Millwall.

6th
Dundee United lose the 1st leg of the UEFA Cup Final going down 1-0 to IFK Gothenburg.... Mark Dennis fined £600 by the FA for bringing the game into disrepute for the third time this season, following newspaper remarks made about Chris Nicholl.... Middlesbrough return to the Second Division, despite being held to a goalless draw in front of 18,500 fans at Ayresome Park.... Aldershot draw 3-3 with champions Northampton and move closer to a play-off position.... Rochdale, not so long ago favourites to drop out of the League, save themselves with a 2-1 win over Stockport. Burnley, Tranmere, Torquay and Lincoln are now the four candidates for the drop to the GM League.

8th
Aston Villa sack Billy McNeill.... Tranmere guarantee themselves League soccer by beating Exeter 1-0 in front of a 6,000 crowd, their largest for more than 10 years.... Southend assure themselves of the third promotion place from Division Four with a 2-0 win at Stockport County.

SAINT: *Well done Tranny and Southend – Big Billy, you hadn't a prayer*

9th
Paul Dobson's goal 30 seconds from the end of the match for Torquay against Crewe means that Lincoln City are bottom of the Fourth Division for just 30 seconds all season and, because of this, lose their League status. Lincoln lose at Swansea while Burnley beat Orient in front of a massive 16,000 crowd.... Elsewhere, Manchester City lose 2-0 at West Ham and are doomed to the Second Division, as are Leicester, who can only draw at Oxford.... Charlton, however, are thrown a lifeline after beating QPR 2-1, and must now engage in the play-offs.... Derby are Second Division champions after beating Plymouth 4-2, and Ipswich join Leeds and Oldham in the play-offs.... Sunderland's home defeat by Barnsley means they have to take part in the play-offs at the bottom of the division.... Gillingham, for so long title contenders in the Third Division, beat Bolton 1-0 and guarantee themselves the final play-off slot, along with Swindon and Wigan, while Bolton are doomed to a play-off at the other end of the table.... Aldershot lose 2-1 at home to Cardiff, but just make the play-off because of Orient's defeat at Burnley.... In Scotland, Rangers wind up their season with a 1-0 win over Cup finalists St Mirren, while Celtic lose 1-0 at Hearts.... Burton Albion and Kidderminster Harriers draw FA Challenge Trophy at Wembley.

10th
On the continent, Diego Maradona's Napoli win the Italian title for the first time.

GREAVSIE: *Diego for Pope!*

11th
With six months of his contract to run, Dave Bassett resigns from Wimbledon.... Cup finalists Spurs field a team of 10 reserves against Everton at Goodison, but still only lose 1–0.

12th
Kidderminster beat Burton 2–1 in Challenge Trophy replay at West Brom. Former Everton 'keeper Jim Arnold saves a Burton penalty three minutes from time.

13th
Johan Cruyff's Ajax beat Lokomotiv Leipzig 1–0 to win the European Cup Winners' Cup.... Coventry's youngsters give hope to the senior squad by beating Charlton 1–0 to win the FA Youth Cup 2–1 on aggregate.... Alan Ball given a £15,000 pay rise as reward for getting Pompey back into the First Division.

14th
In the 1st legs of the play-offs, Leeds beat Oldham 1–0 in front of 29,000 fans, while Ipswich are held at home to a goalless draw by Charlton.... Gillingham beat Sunderland 3–2, thanks to a Cascarino hat-trick, and Wigan lose at home to Swindon by the same score.... Aldershot, who only just made the play-offs, beat Bolton 1–0 and Colchester lose at home to Wolves by two goals to nil.... There are 90 applicants for the post of manager of Lincoln City, including Trevor Cherry and Alex Stepney.

SAINT: *Can you believe it?*

16th
Coventry beat Spurs 3–2 after extra time in a classic Cup Final.... St Mirren beat Dundee United 1–0, also after extra time.... Michel Platini announces his retirement because he is 'no longer enjoying the game'.

17th
Charlton keep their hopes of First Division football alive by beating Ipswich 2–1 and Leeds earn the right to meet them in the final, despite losing 2–1 at Oldham in front of 19,000. Leeds win on the away goals rule.... It is, however, a sad day for Sunderland. Over 25,000 fans pack into Roker Park to see them win a seven-goal thriller, but Gillingham win on the away goals.... Swindon beat Wigan 3–2 on aggregate, the score from the 1st leg.... Aldershot pull off one of the shocks of the play-offs by dooming Bolton to the Fourth Division.... 16,000 at Molineux watch Wolves beat Colchester.... In the Welsh Cup Final non-League Merthyr Tydfil hold Newport to a 2–2 draw; Bob Latchford scores one of the goals for Merthyr.

18th
Graham Taylor quits Watford and takes charge of Aston Villa, while Dave Bassett fills the vacancy at Vicarage Road.... Rangers agree to pay Tel Aviv Macabbi £100,000 for Avi Cohen, former Liverpool team-mate of Graeme Souness.... Southampton give a free transfer to their 32-year-old captain Nick Holmes, who has been at the Dell 17 years and played 542 times for the first team.

19th
England and Brazil draw 1–1 at Wembley in the Rous Cup in front of 92,000 fans....

Chelsea sign England Under-21 full back Tony Dorigo from Aston Villa for £400,000.

GREAVSIE: *Brazil – you were lucky! Wonder how your lot will get on against them, Saint?*

20th
Dundee United draw 1–1 with IFK Gothenburg but lose the UEFA Cup 2–1 on aggregate ... Bobby Ferguson's contract as manager of Ipswich not renewed.... Mick McCarthy joins Celtic from Manchester City for £500,000, a record fee for the Scottish club.

21st
Arsenal sign Wimbledon full back Nigel Winterburn for £400,000.... Mel Machin appointed Manchester City's new team manager, with Jimmy Frizzell becoming general manager.... Gordon Milne quits his post of Leicester City general manager.

22nd
Manchester United pay £250,000 for Arsenal and England full back Viv Anderson.... In the play-offs, Gillingham beat Swindon 1–0 in their 1st leg match. The crowd is 16,775.... Aldershot beat Wolves 2–0.

23rd
Jim Melrose scores for Charlton three minutes from time as they beat Leeds 1–0 in their play-off match before a crowd of 16,680.... Scotland and England play out a boring 0–0 draw in the Rous Cup match at Hampden.... Liam Brady scores the only goal of the match as the Republic of Ireland beat Brazil 1–0 in a friendly.

SAINT: *England not as good as you thought, James!*

24th
A crowd of 58,000 sees Mansfield Town beat Bristol City to win the Freight Rover Trophy at Wembley. The score after extra time is 1–1 and the first Wembley final to be decided on penalties is resolved when Tony Kenworthy hits home the 12th spot kick of the shoot-out.

25th
Nearly 20,000 Wolves fans numbed as their side lose at home to Aldershot in the play-offs.... A crowd of 31,395 at Elland Road sees Leeds beat Charlton 1–0, so drawing 1–1 on aggregate; they must play again, as must Swindon and Gillingham who draw 2–2 on aggregate.

26th
Brazil give a classy performance to beat Scotland 2–0 at Hampden and win the Rous Cup.

GREAVSIE: *I'll repeat that score – Scotland 0 Brazil 2*

27th
FC Porto come from behind to beat Bayern Münich 2–1 in a classic European Cup Final in Vienna.... John Bond dismissed by Birmingham City.

28th
The Republic of Ireland beat Luxembourg 2–0 in the European Championship.... Celtic dismiss manager David Hay and recall former manager and player Billy McNeill.... Gary Pendrey, Wolves' assistant manager since November, appointed manager of his old club, Birmingham City.

29th
Charlton come from behind with two Peter Shirtliff goals in extra time against Leeds United to retain First Division status. They win 2–1.... Swindon beat Gillingham 2–0 to reach the Second Division under Lou Macari, the man the Swindon directors sacked then reinstated two years ago.

SAINT AND GREAVSIE: *It's hats off to Lennie and Lou!*

Getting carried away ... Clive Allen of Spurs gets lift-off from Coventry's Trevor Peake in the friendly FA Cup Final of 1987

2

Singing the Blues

Jimmy Greaves

The Blues - Everton and Coventry City - were the big winners of season 1986-7 - Everton as champions, City as shock winners of the FA Cup. In this chapter Greavsie gives an insight into the story behind the great Everton revival under Howard Kendall and follows up with a personal look at Coventry.

Everton

So Everton won the championship and lost a manager!

Well, I for one wasn't surprised when they overhauled great rivals Liverpool to land the title for the second time in three years ... after all I tipped the Reds and as anyone who watches *Saint and Greavsie* on Saturday mornings will know, that is the kiss of death for any Championship contenders. Saint of course tipped Howard Kendall's men for the Championship although I believe he only did it in order to have a peaceful life. He's a legend at Anfield and now he's got the other half of the city on his side too ... crafty old Jock!

Mind you neither of us could possibly

have tipped Howard Kendall's dramatic departure to sunny Spain ... to say that decision was a shock is an understatement.

What made Howard look for pastures new? I'm sure money and the fresh challenge came into it but, despite the assurances from Everton fans on the day he quit for Bilbao that he would always be welcomed back, I wonder if he, like me, remembered a dark winter's day four years ago when the fans were out for his blood. Did Howard never forgive them for putting himself and his family through several weeks of hell? Was he determined to get out at the top having made the biggest comeback since Lazarus?

I'm not one of life's statisticians but Sunday, 6 November 1983 will forever be indelibly inscribed on my mind. For on that date, Everton and Howard Kendall were down and out ... knackered ... on the soccer

---

Gary glitters ... Lineker on song with one of the golden goals that prompted Barcelona to break the bank for him

scrap heap. And to steal Max Boyce's catchphrase 'I was there'. I remember it well because I was part of one of the bleakest days ever for Goodison fans. Their team was languishing near the bottom of the First Division and they faced Liverpool at Anfield. It was generally felt that, should Everton lose to the Reds, then Howard Kendall would be sacked ... and lose they did in rather spectacular style.

Before an audience of millions on ITV's *Big Match Live*, Liverpool didn't just beat Everton. They took them apart in a way which reminded me of a fish-wife plying her trade in Billingsgate Market. Everton were filleted by Rush and company. The final score was 3–0, but frankly it could have been double figures, and I've seldom seen a team so relieved to hear the final whistle in a derby match as Howard Kendall's men were that day.

It was a massacre. A rout. Everton had only one shot on target in the entire 90 minutes – a 35-yard effort from Graeme Sharp. Their fans, not to put too fine a point on it, were not happy. They roared for Howard Kendall's head and as I left the ground my cap was pulled over my eyes. I would rather have run up against a hungry bear than an Everton fan that afternoon. No one who has had anything to do with football wants to see a manager sacked, but as my thoughts went back to Everton sides of the past, I felt that Howard Kendall had a mission impossible ... to hang on as boss at Goodison.

As I made my way to Radio City for a talk-in radio programme with the Saint and Ron Atkinson, my mind kept flashing back to the sixties and seventies and the quality teams and players which Everton had produced. Goodison, in those days under that great manager Harry Catterick,

was known as the 'School of Science' ... and rightly so. The 'School' produced sweet, skilful teams capable of winning titles and trophies in devastating manner.

In the sixties there were players such as Jimmy Gabriel, the tough-as-teak Scottish wing half who would surge past me urging on his forwards in some of the epic battles Spurs had with his Everton side. There was big Brian Labone, superb in the air, and one of the best examples to any young player on how to conduct oneself on and off the field ... booked only twice in 14 years in senior football ... a tremendous record for any centre half. Tony Kay was a firebrand wing half whose career was cut short by the infamous bribes scandal of the sixties, but whose drive and skill would, I'm sure, have won him much more than the single England cap he achieved against Switzerland.

I remember Alex Parker, the cultured Scottish full back who teamed up with his countryman, that flying winger Alex Scott, to form such a devastating right-side partnership. And on the other side of the defence was the great Ray Wilson, with whom I had the pleasure to play so many times for England. Ray was the ultimate full back ... a true world great. I've often heard it said that his sloppy back header which led to Helmut Haller equalizing England's opening goal in the 1966 World Cup Final was his one and only mistake in an England jersey. It may seem an exaggeration, but I don't remember any others.

Then there was 'The Golden Vision', the great Alex Young – the blond bombshell from Scotland who, in my opinion, apart from Dixie Dean, was the finest centre forward ever to pull on an Everton jersey.

Charisma surrounded Young like a mantle. His shock of blond hair made him stand out like a beacon on foggy Merseyside winter afternoons ... and the man could play. Often I've watched him score a goal out of nothing and thought 'How the hell does he manage it?' Alex was a contemporary of mine and one I held in the highest regard. His graceful, flowing style was a pleasure to watch and the hero worship he received in the Blue quarter of Liverpool was thoroughly deserved.

In the seventies too, Everton progressed with players such as Roger Kenyon, the fine centre half who followed Labone; the great midfield triangle of Howard Kendall, Alan Ball and Colin Harvey who set up so many magic trophy-winning moments with their marvellous midfield skills and

Goodison good guys ... Howard Kendall (left) and chairman Philip Carter revived Everton before peseta power lured the manager to Bilbao

running power; Mick Lyons, another great centre half; and up front those two danger-ous strikers Bob Latchford and Joe Royle. Big Bob's bustling style made him a con-stant threat to opposing defences and Joe, to my mind, was one of the finest centre forwards NEVER to win an abundance of England caps. A great header of the ball, he won only six full caps for his country and I for one could never fathom why.

As I headed towards the Radio City phone-in studio, other Everton names from the past flitted through my mind: Derek Temple ... Gordon West ... Mike Trebilcock ... Tommy Wright ... Fred Pickering ... Johnny Morrissey – all players in the classic Everton mould. As I cast my mind back to the afternoon shambles at Anfield I thought, 'What the hell has happened? This lot couldn't lace their boots.'

I must admit I was a little apprehensive going on the air on *The Saint on Sunday* programme. After all, there was I, an out-sider, a simple Londoner about to sit in on a wake – at least Atko was from the Mid-lands. In retrospect the programme wasn't bad ... IT WAS HORRIFIC!

I had made my mind up to try to gain sympathy for Howard and explain to all those nice people about the problems of management and how they should remember the great things he had done for Everton as a player. I soon realized that my task was not an easy one. In fact, I had as much chance of winning sympathy for Howard as Arthur Scargill had of becom-ing prime minister!

Abusive was not the word. Caller after caller demanded Howard's head and they weren't bothering about any silver platter. All Everton's ills were down to Kendall according to the Goodison faithful and they didn't half let Saint, Ron Atkinson, myself and a few million listeners know it. I have to admit that my defence rested very early on in the one-sided discussion.... I'm not daft and anyway I had my car parked outside the radio station and I wanted it still in one piece when I got out.

Seriously though, that phone-in was one of the most embarrassing hours of my life. The whole of Liverpool was listening in and most of Manchester, too. To show how ridiculous it all got, one fan asked, 'Why don't you take the job?' I asked, 'Is it Saint or Ron you're talking to?' 'No,' came the reply. 'It's you Greavsie!' – now I ask you....

We three so-called broadcasters could only sit back and look at one another in disbelief at the venom that was being spilled over the airwaves. Now, I'm no prude, but even with the delay censor local radio stations use in live phone-ins, the language was choice ... and the vitriol was all aimed at one man – Howard Kendall. I've seldom been more relieved to finish any broadcast and at the end of the show Saint, Big Ron and myself shook our heads. If there had ever been doubts that Howard was on his way, surely this radio programme had dispelled them.

I headed off down the motorway for the quiet of Essex wondering just how the press would treat the Kendall situation the next day and just how long it would be before the chop came. The next day, of course, the headlines blazed out the grim news 'EVERTON IN CRISIS'; 'KENDALL ON HIS WAY?'; 'BLUES SHAMED AGAIN'. It seemed that Howard Kendall's career as Everton manager could be measured in hours, not days, that it was all over bar the shouting for the man who had given his all both as player and manager for the Blues.

But then nothing happened. The fatal chairman's 'vote of confidence', the death knell for so many bosses, never came and much to everyone's amazement Kendall was allowed to soldier on, reprieved it seemed by a single goal victory over Nottingham Forest the following Saturday. Adrian Heath was the scorer.

It was then that one of those little bits of magic which sometimes touch football occurred. Those same players who had taken such a thrashing from Liverpool on that fateful November day suddenly started winning ... and winning ... and winning.

The Derek Mountfields, the Kevin Sheedys, the Peter Reids, the Graeme Sharps and the John Baileys began to believe in their own abilities again and with the purchase of that craggy Scot Andy Gray, and the emergence of Neville Southall as an international goalkeeper, Everton were suddenly, surprisingly, on the march again and with a team of quality coached by Kendall's old midfield mate Colin Harvey who of course is now Everton's manager. The rest is history and really if there has been a 'Roy of the Rovers' story in football at the highest level that season surely saw it.

From that dismal November day Everton went on to reach the Milk Cup Final against old rivals Liverpool. This time there was no slaughter, only a grimly fought Wembley final which ended 0-0, followed by an almost as tight replay at Maine Road, where only a superb Graeme Souness goal made the difference between the two teams. Everton and Howard Kendall had made their point.... Liverpool might be still the Kings of Merseyside, but those 'Easy, Easy' days for Reds fans were coming to an end. The Blues followed up their Milk Cup Final appearance by going back to Wembley for the FA Cup, and goals by Graeme Sharp and the ultra-influential Andy Gray were enough to see off a plucky, but outclassed Watford.

As I sat in ITV's Wembley studio that day I couldn't help thinking back to that radio phone-in. How many of the fans who cheered players and manager alike around Wembley had put the Timpsons in earlier in the season? It brought back a smashing piece of homespun philosophy once told to me by the wife of my old Tottenham mate Alan Gilzean after Spurs fans had turned on Gillie and me when one of our little penalty box moves had broken down. 'That sums football up,' she said, 'forty thousand experts watching twenty-two idiots.' I think that just about sums up the pressures of management.

It's the one big job where you have to please all of the people all of the time ... except perhaps if you are lucky enough to have a chairman as loyal as Philip Carter. Carter is one of the quiet men of football. He doesn't hog the headlines or make ludicrous demands of players or coaches, but I believe the whole of football could learn from his style of management. Let's face it, it was Carter who stood behind Kendall in his darkest days and look at the benefits he and his club are reaping now. I only hope UEFA see fit to lift the ban on English fans soon, for I honestly feel that Everton can carry on the great revival and lift the European Cup.

It should be noted that it is the managers who were shown loyalty whose clubs gained success in season 1986–7. Wimbledon and Watford, two of my teams of the season, gained high League and Cup placings under Dave Bassett and Graham Taylor ... both these managers will be sadly missed at these clubs in the new season. Likewise ex-Everton hero Joe Royle, whose Oldham Athletic only just missed out on promotion, and Arthur Cox who repaid Derby County with the Second Division title. And last but not least, little Lou Macari who repaid the Swindon directors big enough to swallow their pride two years ago by reinstating him after firing him, by giving them a seat in the Second Division directors' boxes this term.

If I digress from the Everton story it is because I firmly believe that Philip Carter set a pattern four years ago by standing behind Kendall. Some have taken the hint, but there is a long way to go before the majority of chairmen realize that success doesn't come overnight and that sacking a manager after only a year or so in charge is not the way to glory. Two championships, an FA Cup and a Cup Winners' Cup surely prove my point.

Some say that Kendall let Carter down by moving on to Bilbao. I believe that to be utter rubbish.

Philip Carter stuck by Kendall and was repaid in full. Kendall like any other individual has a right to seek the best security possible for both himself and his family. It was a brave move by Kendall and only time will tell whether it was a correct one but let no one say that he didn't pay his dues at Goodison ... the honours list tells the true story.

But what of Everton's future under Colin Harvey? Colin is one of the quiet men of football but people who know say that he has been a major influence in the Blues revival. Pulled out of the Goodison youth set-up to help Kendall in his darkest days, he has instilled both skill and confidence into Everton, and his four years as Kendall's right-hand man will have prepared him for the job.

And whisper it, but I always rated Harvey the 'thinker' in that marvellous Kendall-Harvey-Ball triangle of the sixties. Colin to me was the intuitive play-maker while the other two were the grafters. And from what I hear he is also an innovatory coach and since there is no reason not to believe that he has learned much under Howard then he should prove the ideal successor.

He should take a tip from Kendall, for Howard learned in his six years as Goodison boss to blend youth with experience ... and his buys in the past four years have been excellent. I think Howard's early 'iffy' buys – players from the Second Division – were due to his inexperience as a manager at top level. When he joined the Blues from Blackburn he fancied he could turn good Second Division players into good First Division ones. ... It doesn't always happen, as many a boss has found out to his cost.

Andy Gray was a gem of a buy from Wolves. I'm sure Andy's knee is like a sack of gold coins. It's been so badly damaged, he must jingle when he walks, but he grabbed his last big chance as a player and not only finished with League Cup and Cup Winners' Cup medals at Goodison, but also added confidence to a side which needed it badly. Andy, to my mind, was too brave for his own good, but that was his nature and the £250,000 Kendall spent on him must go down as one of the buys of the century.

Andy, of course, became a Goodison hero

and will eventually become a legend in Blues history. But it's worth noting that Kendall had the courage to sell him after the initial job was done ... and then came Lineker. Gary had impressed me for several seasons at Leicester City, yet only Howard Kendall recognized his potential. A season later he was on his way to Barcelona, but Everton had £3 million in the bank.

The transfer money from Lineker's move has been well spent – on Dave Watson from Norwich, to help stabilize the defence; and Ian Snodin from Leeds United to pep up the attack ... and that signing against fierce opposition from Liverpool. Snodin upset Kenny Dalglish by saying that he chose Goodison rather than Anfield because he felt that Everton would have further success ... by implication, more than Liverpool. Well, it's early days but one Championship medal is already in the Snodin trophy cabinet. These were two fine signings and I'm sure there are more to come. To my mind Everton in season 1986-7 established themselves as a club that is going to be around the honours list for a long time to come.

I've touched on the signings of Watson and Snodin, good First Division players, but let's not forget the players who have been at Goodison some time now, but who nevertheless are still relatively young men. Neville Southall, recovered from his ankle break, is as good as ever and in my opinion is now the best goalkeeper in Britain. Peter Shilton has had a fair innings, but Southall's day has arrived. Neville is not a flashy 'keeper but is super-efficient. I remember towards the end of the season, with Championship and relegation at stake, the Everton–Manchester City match at Goodison where City had their tails up

Just champion! Gary Stevens (2) salutes Pat Van Den Hauwe as one of Pat's rare goals clinches Everton's title at Norwich

and Southall kept his goal intact with some superb stops ... and potential disaster was turned into a golden point *en route* to the title. He had many more days like that in a superb season.

Like every class side, the Everton team is settling into a pattern. The Stevens boys, Gary and Trevor, when fit, are automatic first-team players these days: two fine signings and now fully established England internationals. Trevor Steven had a dull season compared to the last Championship-winning campaign, but I feel he has the potential to become one of England's biggest stars. His scorching right-wing pace will trouble any full back and he can combine his high speed skills with bullet-like strikes from the most unlikely positions.

At the back Kevin Ratcliffe has all the speed, poise and aggression needed to kill off any sudden counter-attack, and he is ably backed up by Pat Van Den Hauwe, who had the pleasure of scoring the goal that won Everton the title at Norwich.

In midfield the constant pushing of Peter Reid (didn't he look younger in 1986–7 with his new black hair?) and the clever promptings of Kevin Sheedy will always be a threat to opposing defences and what forward would not thrive on their service? The search for cultured midfield players is endless, so I often wonder how Liverpool feel when they watch Sheedy conduct play with all the skill of an orchestra leader ... after all, they lost him to the Blues for a mere £100,000 (a figure set by the tribunal) in 1982.

Up front I've always been a believer in partnerships. I had Bobby Smith and Alan Gilzean alongside me at Tottenham, and when you think back over the years all the great teams have had their double acts too. For me Graeme Sharp and Adrian Heath come into that mould. Heath, the impish, quicksilver, audacious little terrier who can conjure a goal out of nothing and Sharp, the tall, physical, target man who can give the biggest and bravest centre halves nightmares. It says much for Everton that they won last season's title without the benefit of that partnership for most of the season because of Sharp's bad injury.

Yet once again Kendall proved himself a manager supreme. A skilful piece of buying saw Wayne Clarke move from Molineux to Goodison (shades of Andy Gray) and Wayne, brother of former Leeds and England star Allan, made an immediate impact. Indeed, it was Wayne's goal against Arsenal at Highbury late in the season which Howard Kendall rated as the

Bye bye Blues ... Gary Lineker (white shorts) scores his farewell goal for Everton, but Liverpool went on to win the FA Cup in '86

turning-point against Liverpool in the battle for the Championship. Tele-viewers will remember it as a cunning lob from 35 yards out after a faulty clearance from Arsenal 'keeper John Lukic. It was to give Everton a valuable 1–0 away win on the same day that Kenny Dalglish's men fell at home to Wimbledon. At the end of the campaign Howard claimed, 'If I were to pick one moment, one game which convinced me that we were on our way ... that was the one.'

And Wayne did it again with that Charity Shield winner against Coventry at Wembley in August.

Now it's Colin Harvey's Everton ... not Howard Kendall's ... and there's no doubt that Colin has a hard act to follow. But the groundwork has been done by both Kendall AND Harvey. Everton to my mind can only get better ... and that spells danger for the rest of the First Division.

And rest easy Colin ... I promise not to lumber you by tipping Everton for the Championship ... that's unless a large brown envelope is forthcoming from a certain Mr Dalglish!

Coventry City

I once visited a car spares store in Coventry ... you know the set-up – one bloke serving (slowly) and a two-hour wait (compulsory) ... and pinned to the wall between Samantha Fox and Linda Lusardi (what a pleasant thought) was a wooden plaque bearing the legend 'THE IMPOSSIBLE WE CAN ACHIEVE. MIRACLES TAKE A LITTLE LONGER.'

Now I haven't been back to that store since but I have a suggestion for my storekeeper friend: rip down your plaque and replace it with a full facial of another winning pair – my old mate John 'Schnoz' Sillett and big George Curtis. After all,

they've made nonsense of the legend and you'll also have a hat-trick of double acts!

Naturally I've got to be a believer in double acts. They seem to have been part of my life through football and now in television, but surely there can have been few more sensational than Schnoz and George, the new all-singing and dancing management team at Highfield Road.

The IMPOSSIBLE they achieved in 1986–7 – at last giving Coventry City stability in the First Division.

The MIRACLE didn't take much longer – winning the FA Cup in the same season in one of Wembley's never-to-be-forgotten Cup Finals against my old club Tottenham Hotspur.

And whisper it around White Hart Lane, but I was praying for a Coventry win in that Final. For City made the 1986–7 Cup campaign. Like Brighton and Jimmy Melia four years earlier, Coventry under Sillett and Curtis brought fun into the latter stages of the Cup, combining smiles with a fighting brand of football we hadn't experienced for yonks.

Mind you, like Everton in the Championship they did have a plus on all their opponents: I did, of course, tip against them every round ... just as for the past four years in my regular Friday night spot with Central Television, I have tipped them to drop into the Second Division.

I must admit though that tipping against them in their Cup run became a real matter of life and death for me. Schnoz, Big George, the team and whole city of Coventry eventually reckoned (completely wrongly, of course) that my tipping against them was their good luck charm and I was under threat from all of them never to tip the Sky Blues. I never did, of course … and was mobbed by Coventry fans in the friendliest way imaginable following the Cup Final for not putting the curse of Greavsie on their team.

Mind you, it did all get a bit ridiculous. In the end everyone in the Midlands knew that in my heart of hearts I was rooting for City even though I didn't dare tip them – hence my helping to present ITV's Cup Final show clobbered up in Coventry colours, but tipping Spurs!

And although I might be ostracized from White Hart Lane for admitting it, I was out of my chair with the rest of them when Keith Houchen scored with that wonderful diving header to bring Coventry back from the dead to 2–2 and force the game into extra time. The rest is history but it really is worth looking in depth at what the Sillett–Curtis partnership achieved in season 1986–7, for it really was magnificent.

Possibly the first sign the outside world got that Coventry were no longer the pushovers of recent years was when they appeared against a first-class Arsenal side at Highbury in ITV's *Big Match Live*. Arsenal's kids at the time were topping the League and sweeping all before them. Yet Coventry not only took the game to Arsenal but also finished up unlucky, certainly to my mind, not to come away from Highbury with three points. In the end a 0–0 draw was enough to convince millions that City were a team to be reckoned with, and thus it proved.

In fact, what the Sky Blues achieved in the season could prove to be the biggest turnaround in fortunes since a certain Bill Shankly took over a struggling Second Division club called Liverpool. Coventry until season 1986–7 were the habitual Hou-

dinis of First Division football. It is to their eternal credit that since Jimmy Hill grabbed them by their bootlaces and pulled them into the First Division they have never been relegated. They are one of the few teams in League history NEVER to drop back out of the First Division after being promoted. Arsenal, of course, are the only team not to have been relegated from the First, the Gunners being in from the start of the League.

But I tell you what, quite a few Coventry fans have gone as bald as old Schnoz himself over the years as their team has flirted with disaster year-in year-out.

I suppose really it needed two outstanding characters to pull City together … and the City directors certainly chose well in appointing Sillett and Curtis as the men to change their destiny. Curtis as managing director, Sillett as first-team coach and now manager – at first the fusing together of this pair must have seemed as unlikely as twinning Jack Lemmon and Walter Matthau in *The Odd Couple*! Well for Coventry fans they have been just as big a hit. And really you've got to understand the nature of the characters to understand the success.

George was one of the hardest men I ever came across in football. I well remember back in the early seventies, teams turning up at Highfield Road in the bleak midwinter when sheepskins were the order of the day. And Curtis, a super-fit bear of a man, would whistle his way through the front door wearing only a T-shirt! I don't know if George did it to scare the opposition, but I tell you what – it worked. Many a centre forward got the message before he even hit the pitch, and I do mean hit the pitch. George was the sort of centre half who loved to play keepy-uppy with opposing centre forwards. It is rumoured his old

In the bleak midwinter George Curtis would whistle his way through the front door wearing only a T-shirt!

granny has bruises on the shins ... similar to one Mr Ian St John.

Saint tells the story of how Shanks took his entire Liverpool side to Highfield Road for Big George's testimonial match. Now usually those matches are gentle affairs. Five-all draws are in order, with practice match conditions applying ... in other words no real physical contact. But that particular 'friendly' had only just started when the poor old Saint, out to show the fans he was soon to play before a little bit of Scottish ball control, was approached by George with all the finesse of a Panzer tank. Says Saint, 'I woke up being carried off on a stretcher. George was never one to take prisoners, but when I chinned him later about the tackle he said, "It's a man's game Saint," and that from a bloke we were down trying to make a few bob for!'

However, Saint joined Coventry under Noel Cantwell soon after and believe it or not, he and George are still mates today. But this is just typical of the attitude Curtis has insisted on at City. He asks that players give everything and fear no one ... and in Schnoz Sillett he has just the man to back him up.

Now Big John fancies himself as a bit of a ball player ... but I've got news for him.... You were one of the biggest rascals I've ever seen on the pitch – every bit as tough as George himself. In fact, Schnoz, I reckon you kicked as many players as Norman Hunter and Tommy Smith put together!

And I should know ... I was there right at the start in the early days with Chelsea when John and his brother Peter, the former England full back, were the first-team full backs. In fact, Schnoz is my oldest friend in football (some might say my only friend). On the day I joined Chelsea as a 15-year-old in 19 mumble mumble that big

beaming face which filled TV screens on Cup Final day was around.

He and Peter befriended me and they became my bosom, not to mention my boozing, buddies, and we had some hilarious moments. Schnoz always did like a pint, a laugh and a punt ... and not always in that order. We had some memorable days under Ted Drake with Chelsea. We were never a great side, but we did score a lot of goals even though we let almost as many in. We were known in those days as the 'All the best club', for the only instruction we ever got from Ted was an 'All the best' as we took the field!

Now Peter Sillett could play a bit: he could sweep a 40-yard pass and land a ball on a sixpence ... a fine, fine player. John, though, was rather more limited, but a man you would always want on your side. In other words, he would run through a brick wall for Chelsea – and if opposing forwards were barring his way to that wall so be it – for they went too! But Schnoz was always good for a laugh, both on the field and off and I'm sure it's that infectious up-and-at-'em, enjoy yourselves attitude which rubbed off on Coventry City last season.

Not that John couldn't play, of course. He was a good senior player, if just a little on the rough side. He did have his moments though ... and I reckon he scored one of the most spectacular goals I've ever seen in my life – mind you, it was against his own team!

It was in the early days of European football and Chelsea had arranged a friendly with Athletic Bilbao in Spain. On this occasion the rain in Spain didn't stay mainly on the plain. It zeroed in on Bilbao and for two days it swamped the place. When we finally took to the pitch in front of 50,000 football-mad Basques it was fit only

Chelsea set of 1960–61 ... featuring Greavsie (front row, second right), next to 'El Tel' Venables and 'Schnoz' Sillett (back row, second right)

for mud wrestlers. I kid you not, no one could kick the ball more than 15 yards. Because of the conditions there were no real chances for either team ... until Schnoz took a hand late in the second half.

Someone chipped the ball back to the big fellow just inside his own half and Schnoz sensibly, he thought, tried to volley it back to our 'keeper Reg Matthews standing on the edge of the box. Unfortunately for John, and Reg, he connected flush on and the ball whistled 40 yards like a heat-seeking rocket straight past our hapless 'keeper and screamed into our net. It's the first time I've ever known John to be speechless. His

mouth opened and closed like a pet guppy, while the rest of us doubled up with laughter. And the last laugh was on Schnoz – the goal was enough to see us beaten 1–0. Mind you, as usual he came up joking, and he finished up giving us forwards stick for not being able to find the net like him.

On another occasion John and Terry Biddlecombe, the famous National Hunt jockey, joined me for a jar on Grand National day in the Queen's Elm pub in Chelsea. We had got friendly with another great jumps jockey, Josh Gifford, and Schnoz had the word that Honey End, Josh's national mount, was the business.

'Can't get beat,' he assured us, gathering in the readies and investing them with the local Honest Fred. And he would have been right ... if it hadn't been for a horse called Foinavon. For it was 1967, the year of the biggest ever National pile-up.

As we three stooges sat in the Queen's Elm watching the black and white telly, a loose horse ran across the leading pack causing the biggest snarl-up since London's North Circular was laid ... and of course Honey End was one of the worst sufferers. Poor Josh was dislodged as leading fancy after leading fancy piled into one another, though he did manage to get hold of the beast and remount it – but not before Foinavon had gone a distance clear and won at 100-1.

Our money had gone and for a moment big John looked a bit upset. But like one of those little round men you just can't knock over he quickly bounced back, telling Terry and me: 'Never mind lads ... we had a pop ... it's only money ... let's have a pint.'

It's that forget-it-and-get-on-with-it attitude which John has taken into Coventry City. He is a larger-than-life character who believes that anything is possible and it was exactly that attitude he managed to instil into the Sky Blues in League and Cup last season. He did have a fair bit of talent available to him in that fabulous run, though. Coventry to me were a gutsy, workmanlike side with a sprinkling of stars. But their important personalities can play.

Take Steve Ogrizovic – Big Oggy – six foot four of goalkeeping competence and outstanding all season for City. I've already touched on the fact that Peter Shilton is nearing the end of a great career and with Bobby Robson looking for possible successors to Shilts, he could do worse

than look to the Coventry 'keeper. Who will ever forget his late saves against Leeds United in that classic Cup semi-final last season – saves that allowed City eventually to go through to Wembley 3–2 in extra time. The big fellow has assurance stamped all over him and, while Chris Woods seems to be being groomed as England's new number one, Big Oggy should be given his chance.

There are two other players in Coventry's line-up who excite me: Cyrille Regis and Dave Bennett. Cyrille in my opinion has always been one of the best strikers in England football. Big, brave and with high-speed skill ability he came back to his best last season and should surely be given another chance for his country. Bobby Robson was at Wembley to watch him tease Richard Gough and company in the

Star in stripes ... Cyrille Regis powers past Chris Hughton to get in another strike on Spurs' goal at Wembley

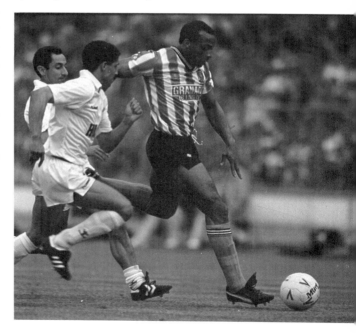

middle of the Spurs defence. I hope the memory hasn't faded in the months that have followed. Cyrille had a few lacklustre seasons, but the appetite is back and with his talent he'll score goals at any level.

And what about Bennett? If he isn't an exciting player then I've never scored a goal. Dave is a throwback to the exciting times of the sixties when a player loved to run at defences, send them sprawling and then still be willing to take a chance himself at the end of it all. His equalizing goal to bring the score to 1–1 at Wembley in the Cup Final was one to remember. So give Dave a chance too, Bobby … he won't let anyone down … the lad can play.

But, of course, Coventry's Cup win wasn't just about three players. Every man on the pitch at Wembley, and others too, did his bit in memorable victories over Manchester United, Sheffield Wednesday and Leeds United to get the club to the twin towers.

The Final itself was surely one of the greatest ever, with both teams going flat out from start to finish. I've never been present at a better one. Mind you, as a Coventry sympathizer on the day, my heart went to my boots when Clive Allen slammed in his 49th of the season to put Spurs ahead after only two minutes.

It's worth recording, by the way, that I thought Clive did a magnificent job for Spurs during the season. I've always fancied the lad as a striker and I was delighted that he broke my old Spurs scoring records in the end. Let's face it, records are only made to be broken anyway.

His start gave Tottenham just the boost they needed and for 10 minutes or so I thought that Coventry might just crumble. But it was then that the steel fired into them by Sillett and Curtis showed. The City lads showed all the grit of true Cup fighters by giving as good as they got and Spurs' pretty patterns were upset.

Suddenly everyone in the Stadium realized that we were in for one of the Cup Finals of the century and it was no real surprise when Dave Bennett scored that marvellous equalizer, pulling the Spurs defence apart before sliding the ball home. It was at this time the City fans gave me a rendering of 'Are you watching, Jimmy Greaves?' – well I was, but who wasn't as the action went on fast and furious.

It was around this point that I felt Chris Waddle was going to rip Coventry apart. Waddle to me always looks absolutely knackered … but Chris is deceptive. He can saunter up to any full back, jink past him and be off like an outside hare at a dog track. Poor Greg Downs must have felt like an also-ran as the big Geordie hoodwinked him again and again. And when Brian Kilcline got his toe to one cross just before Gary Mabbutt made contact, Ogrizovic was beaten to the world and Spurs were 2–1 ahead … an own goal to their rescue and the promise of more to come. But after the interval they didn't exploit Waddle the man who looked at one stage ready to make Wembley all his own.

Back came Coventry and when Keith Houchen dived to score one of the best Cup Final goals ever, I had a feeling that the ribbons on the old trophy were set to be

Top: Headlong into history … Keith Houchen's Wembley wonder flies past Spurs keeper Ray Clemence and Coventry are on their way to a 3–2 victory

Sky Blue heaven … that upcoming comedy duo Curtis (left) and Sillett on cloud nine with one of Coventry's cup heroes, goalscorer Dave Bennett

coloured sky blue. As it was, the extra-time own goal by Gary Mabbutt was a tragic way to decide a fantastic match in which every Spurs man played his part too, but it should be remembered that Big Cyrille and Micky Gynn (twice) could have made sure. The Cup, though, was Coventry's. The impossible had happened, and the team who had started the Cup campaign as 66–1 outsiders were suddenly part of football history ... and rightly so.

Yet strangely the success Coventry had last season may mean that some of the players who etched their names into Highfield Road history may be forced to move on. For Cup runs mean money. And the cash which has flowed into the City coffers means that suddenly Sillett and Curtis find themselves with the funds to improve the team, the cash to speculate on new players. And they will buy, for progress is the name of the game and it is vital that Coventry now go on to build a new future. Fresh talent, forged together with the exciting youngsters who won the FA Youth Cup, offer Sky Blues fans years of good times ahead and I'm sure the City bosses will not flinch when it comes to improvement.

But even moving on won't diminish the magic of Coventry's greatest-ever day. The players who took part in the 1987 Cup Final win over Spurs will never forget their moment of glory – the victory lap, the sky-blue toppers, the banners and the songs will be etched on every player's mind.

And I've a confession to make – it will be forever etched on mine too. I admit to having a lump in my throat as the Coventry lads jigged their way round Wembley. My fun with them throughout the season, as well as my close friendship with John Sillett, meant I wanted them to win that Cup almost more than I wanted any other thing in football. In fact, I reckon I was more excited at Coventry winning their trophy than I was when my Spurs team won against Chelsea at Wembley in 1967 ... and that's saying something.

Coventry on that day were not only a credit to themselves and their city but also to football. I'm certain that the 1987 Cup Final will go down as one of the greatest ever. It must rank with the Stanley Matthews Final of 1953, the Mike Trebilcock Final of 1966, and the Ricky Villa final of 1982.

Spurs, of course, played their part in making it great, but in the end the day belonged to the Sky Blues, Big George and Schnoz – and, of course, to those marvellous, patient, long-suffering fans. And I've news for them: you may have had to wait 104 years for your first major success but I'm willing to bet the bad times are over – like Everton, there's more to come.

3

Sweet Tony Adams ... and Others

Ian St John

The gospel according to St John is that the 12 young men he has selected in this chapter are set to become the football superstars of tomorrow. His Dynamic Dozen consists of some players you will know, others you will not. But Ian is insistent. They will grace the battlefronts of international soccer.

Like fine wine, football can have its bad and its good years. Some seasons are lit up with an array of exciting talent, goals and incidents. Others seem plagued with uninspired football, stereotyped tactics and lacklustre talent. But when the soccer historians look back on season 1986-7, they may well tag it as a vintage year in British football, and not just because of the exploits of such as Everton, Coventry, Arsenal, Rangers, Dundee United and St Mirren. For season 1986-7 was the year of the young ones, the year exciting young talent

Tony Adams' defensive class with Arsenal brought back memories of Bobby Moore at his England best

exploded on to the British football scene with all the ferocity of a meteorite.

In the days of Greavsie and myself the talent was abundant, but not many players hit the headlines in their early teens: Denis Law, George Best, Duncan Edwards and Greavsie himself were exceptions rather than the rule. But nowadays I find it amazing just how many kids are thrown in at, say, 17 or 18 and quickly establish themselves for life as outstanding players. And season 1986-7's young stars have that look of permanency about them. I realize that much can go wrong in a footballer's formative years, but if ever a batch of players looked destined for long careers in the hurly-burly of league and international football it was this lot.

There was so much young talent about, and I'm talking about right down the leagues, that it is perhaps a little unfair to single out any for special attention, but these are my tips for the top, the stars of the future, the kids each country will look to in the European Championships and World Cups of tomorrow.

Where better to start than with the young man who in England collected more rave notices than any other – Tony Adams of Arsenal and England, the Fiat Uno Young Player of the Year. George Graham of Arsenal had a bumper harvest of young players in his Littlewoods Cup-winning season – no less than three of his bright young men were nominated for the monthly Fiat Uno awards, but it was Adams who captured the imagination of the judges and England manager Bobby Robson with performances hallmarked with confidence.

It was difficult at times to believe that Adams was only 20 years old, as he marshalled the Gunners' defence with all the maturity of a seasoned professional against the top teams in the land. His blond hair and lithe, athletic style quickly had him tagged as 'the new Bobby Moore' – a compliment indeed when one remembers the outstanding skills of England's World Cup-winning captain. Normally I would hesitate to brand any youngster as having the style of such a high-calibre predecessor, but in Adams' case I have to admit that there is so much in his play which reminds me of Moore in his heyday. Bobby was a world-class player – cool, commanding, athletic and brave – a natural leader of men. Tony Adams to me has the same outstanding abilities. He shows tremendous maturity and, not only has he managed to break into the Arsenal team and hold his place, but he is now recognized as a regular member of Bobby Robson's full international squad ... a fabulous achievement for his age.

Tony, I'm sure, has a great future with England ahead of him. A good reader of the game, he always attempts to use the ball when breaking from defence and is commanding in the air as well as tough in the tackle. He's been given his head by George Graham and has thrived on the responsibility. There is no doubt in my mind that he will be a cornerstone of Arsenal and England teams for many years to come. A tremendous prospect.

Likewise, so is his Highbury team-mate David Rocastle, the Michael Jackson lookalike whose performances throughout the season impressed friend and foe alike. To me, Rocastle is one of the most exciting young players to hit the First Division for some time. A natural athlete, David has marvellous close control, moves well on the ball and likes to take defenders on. Who will ever forget his outstanding performances

David Rocastle helped Arsenal to the top, supplying ammunition for the Littlewoods Cup winners' strikers

in those exciting Littlewoods Cup semi-final matches against Tottenham?

Rocastle on those occasions sparkled like a gem in the mud of Highbury and White Hart Lane as he ran his heart out to give his team fresh life in a tie which seemed to have slipped out of their grasp. Time and again David would thrust down the right wing, ever ready to turn the Spurs defenders before driving in the crosses which just begged to be buried in the Tottenham net.

He can score goals, too. It was he who scored the winner against Tottenham in the Littlewoods Cup semi-final replay – the goal that sent Arsenal on their way to Wembley and final victory over Liverpool. But the lad will always score goals. He is one of those rare players these days who is always prepared to try things inside the penalty box and, if the chance comes, is selfish enough to have a go. Rocastle, like Tony Adams, seemed to grow in stature with Arsenal as the season progressed.

It was a long and arduous season for the Gunners youngsters but they came through it with honours and their long spell at the top of the League, the Littlewoods Cup victory and the disappointing defeat by Watford in the FA Cup were all part of the learning process. Adams and Rocastle will be the better for it, as will the other Arsenal strikers.

In Rocastle, Arsenal have another England star of the future, I'm certain of that. In fact, such was David's progress in his first full year as a first-team player that I would not be surprised if Bobby Robson gave him the same chance he gave Tony Adams. Certainly there is no doubt in my mind that David Rocastle is a player whom England fans will savour in the years to come.

I've talked a lot about Tony Adams being in the mould of Bobby Moore, and it's strange how many of season 1986–7's players remind me of so many great players of the past. For someone like myself who remembers well the fine Leeds United team of the late sixties and early seventies, there is a sense of *déjà vu* when I watch Everton these days. For Wayne Clarke not only looks like his brother Allan 'Sniffer' Clarke of Leeds and England, he plays like him, too.

Clarke may yet go down in history as one of Howard Kendall's finest (and cheapest!) signings. Bought from Birmingham last season in the midst of Everton's injury crisis, Wayne quickly established himself as a first-team regular with a series of performances which made one wonder why he had languished in Second Division football for so long. His brother Allan gained his nickname because of his ability to sniff a goal out of nothing; and Wayne has that same uncanny ability of all good strikers – to be in the right place at the right time.

Greavsie in this book mentions the goal Howard Kendall believes turned the title Everton's way in season 1986–7, the Wayne Clarke chip from 35 yards after John Lukic made a bad clearance. I think that delicate effort proved that Wayne has every bit as much of a nose for a goal as Sniffer himself. I'm sure Wayne's career will blossom with Everton – he is a player in the Goodison mould. He's the type of player who can take a ball to feet at speed, cushion it, and then dispatch a colleague with a fine through-ball. He has great ability and is a fine link-up player. Everton's style is to build quickly with close passing from midfield and Wayne, apart from his striking abilities, has the natural talent to play that kind of game. He likes to bring other players into the game, and with Everton's style of play that is most important.

In fact, Colin Harvey's biggest problem this term will be whom to leave out to accommodate Clarke. I'm certain he will be even better this term than last and he could be a major figure at Goodison in years to come: definitely a young man to watch in the future. Will he turn out to be as good or better than big brother Allan? Only time will tell ... but Wayne certainly has the potential.

My next selection is a young man Wayne Clarke will almost certainly find himself up against in the years to come, goalkeeper Gary Walsh of Manchester United. Now United fans have not had a lot to cheer about in the past couple of years but knowing Alex Ferguson as I do, the success the Old Trafford fans expect may be just around the corner. And since success is built on good foundations, where better to start than in the 'keeper position? Certainly Gary Walsh in my opinion is one for the future both at club and international level. Young Gary was thrown in at the deep end by Ferguson during the latter stages of the League campaign, mainly because of the serious injury which ended the career of England goalkeeper Gary Bailey. Rarely have I seen a young man grab his chance with both hands so effectively. I watched him on several occasions and he had the ice-cool look which all goalkeepers of quality possess. He is lithe, tall and has an eye for the unexpected.

I remember well watching him at Old Trafford in the crucial last weeks of the Championship against a Liverpool side intent on retaining their title. You cannot get a much tougher game for any young player. The crowd, the atmosphere and the tension can panic senior players, never

mind the kids. But young Gary took it all in his stride. He remained as cool as a cucumber, handled everything Liverpool threw at him like a veteran, and won the respect of United and Liverpool fans alike. And he had one real moment of glory – a tremendous save from Craig Johnston with the score 0–0. That kept United in the match and in the end a late goal from Peter Davenport gave them three points and

Teenage 'keeper Gary Walsh took over from the unfortunate Gary Bailey between the sticks at Old Trafford

Liverpool a defeat they were never really to recover from.

So look out for Gary Walsh. He's a young man who I'm certain is ready to follow in the tradition of outstanding Manchester goalkeepers ... and how good it is to see a young man of promise in the hottest position of all. I wonder if he has a Scottish granny?

Talking about the Scots, don't believe that because internationally we were a disaster in 1986–7 there is no outstanding young talent north of the border ... far from it. My spies in Scotland tell me that fresh, exciting talent is to be found in abundance but that we might have to wait a few years before it is ready to hit the international scene.

One man who shouldn't have to wait too much longer, though, is Derek Ferguson of Rangers. Ferguson played a major part in the Ibrox club's winning two out of three of the major trophies in Scotland last season ... the Skol League Cup and the Fine Fare Premier League Championship. Alongside Graeme Souness and Iain Durrant in midfield, he has emerged as a player of real quality for Rangers.

I've kept an eye on Derek for several years now and he seems to get better every time I watch him. He is quick, a ball winner and loves to go forward, and he has that little bit of magic which to my mind sets him apart from others. For Derek possesses that unique ability which was used to such great effect by one of his Ibrox predecessors, my old Scotland team-mate Jim Baxter – the ability to turn a game with one rapier-like pass into the penalty area. My old boss Bill Shankly used to say of Baxter: 'He can hit a crafty ball, a cunning pass ... and if the defence is not up to him, he'll fillet you like a kipper.'

He was right, too – and Ferguson, whom I've admired since he was 16 years old, has that same ability. He's a player in the Baxter mould all right, and there can be no greater praise than that. Baxter was always trying to find his forwards through little gaps in the opposing defence – and he could pierce the stongest of them.

Playing alongside seasoned internationals such as Terry Butcher, Graham Roberts and Souness himself in a Championship-winning side has boosted Derek's confidence. He is constantly putting himself about, probing for the opening to free his front men and his type of play is just what Scotland need. We have been sadly lacking a Baxter-like figure in midfield since Souness called it a day and, since Andy Roxburgh has used the young Ranger in Scotland youth sides, I will be very surprised if he does not introduce him into the full international arena in the World Cup qualifying matches ahead.

He is an exciting talent ... and one which may help Scotland fans forget the dismal time following our World Cup exit. Watch him stake his claim in the Scotland team.

And what price an ex-Motherwell player joining Derek in the Scottish set-up at some time in the future? Under Tommy McLean, my old club established themselves in the Premier League in 1986–7, and that was good for an old die-hard like me to see. But not too many people south of the border will recognize the name I'm now going to suggest could be one of Scotland's striking stars of tomorrow. Yet Andy Walker, the brave young battler who led the Motherwell line so well last term, and was snapped up by Celtic in the close season, is one of my tips for the top.

Motherwell throughout the years have thrown up a clutch of fine centre forwards.

In recent years players such as Joe McBride, later of Celtic, John 'Dixie' Deans, Willie Pettigrew and Brian McClair have all come out of Fir Park – all players capable of winning titles and trophies by virtue of their razor-sharp finishing.

Walker, while last season at times leading a lone charge up front, seems to me to have all the qualities to mature into a player of the same calibre as the ones I've mentioned. Andy perhaps doesn't as yet have the scoring rate of, say, Joe or Dixie

but that I feel was down to Motherwell's style of play. I'm sure that once he settles down at Celtic under Billy McNeill, then the goals will start to flow.

Andy reminds me of another Andy – Andy Gray. Like the old lionheart, he is as tough as nails, very brave and will not be intimidated. He has an excellent tough streak and again is not frightened to go it alone in the box, the sign of a real striker.

Certainly I'll be watching young Andy's future with interest. That Scotland jersey is

Home-grown Derek Ferguson shone alongside Souness and the big-money buys as Rangers rose again

not too far away if he continues to show the same progress as he did last term.

Look out, by the way, for big changes in Scotland's squad. Andy Roxburgh, having gone through a miserable season, has decided that many of the young players who did well for him at youth level should be given their chance. Frankly the youngsters couldn't do any worse than some of the men who wore the dark blue jersey in season 1986-7, which was certainly not a vintage one for we Scots.

From Scotland to Wales, and there's no doubt that the team which Mike England built has made its mark on the international front over the past few years. Their European Championship successes have made them feared by everyone and with Ian Rush and Mark Hughes up front no defence can rest easy against the Red Dragons.

Well, I have bad news for international defences – Big Mike has two more young players up his sleeve who are about to cause you even more problems. The talented duo are Deniol Graham of Manchester United and Malcolm Allen of Watford, both products of their clubs' youth schemes, and being tipped by Mike England as international stars of the future.

Only the avid Manchester United faithful will know of Graham, but it seems certain that the whole of British football will know of him before long. Still only 17, he has already played in the Welsh Youth side and, according to England, is another Ian Rush ... and that has got to be some recommendation from a man who knows Rush so well.

Says Mike: 'In Welsh terms he is another Rushie, in your terms he is another Denis Law. He has electrifying pace, great vision and can snap up the chances. His progress is exciting. I'm certain that if he continues to improve he is going to give us one of the most lethal attacks in international football.'

Mike's judgement is also backed up by the Manchester United backroom staff. It is perhaps too early to lumber the boy, but already some are saying that he is one of the most exciting young talents on the United books since the early days of George Best. Young Deniol is obviously one to look out for – and don't be too surprised if Mike England gives him his full international chance at only 17. Shades of Denis Law indeed!

Malcolm Allen is, I'm sure, going to be another winner for Wales. A Graham Taylor discovery at Watford, Malcolm has already made his debut for his country and he strikes me as a young player going places fast. At the moment he plays up front for Watford and he has also played there for Wales but many see his future in midfield, as he lacks a little pace.

A fine athlete, Malcolm is another like David Rocastle who is not afraid to take on opposing defences. ITV viewers may remember him as the young man who came on as a substitute for Watford in their FA Cup tie at Vicarage Road last season and made an immediate impact. Watford eventually went through to the next round courtesy of a Luther Blissett birthday goal, but in the short time he was on the pitch Malcolm looked a player of potential. Like Rocastle he is improving all the time and he reminds me a little of another man who loved to run full pelt at opposing defences, my old mate Mike Channon. I've watched Malcolm on several occasions and he has the poise and balance of a good player plus the vision essential at top international level.

Battling for success. . . Ally McCoist (Rangers) and Gary Mabbutt (Tottenham) set
the pattern in a pre-season friendly at White Hart Lane

Above: Play it again Clive. Spurs' record scorer gives his club a dream start to the F.A. Cup Final at Wembley

Left: The equaliser coming up. . .and Coventry's Dave Bennett leaves Gary Mabbutt stranded

Above right: Gary gets his own back. . .and Spurs are back in the lead with a little help from Coventry's Brian Kilcline

Right: Keith Houchen dives to score one of Wembley's greatest Cup Final goals. It's 2-2 and extra time looms

t: And its final tragedy for
ry Mabbutt. His own goal
es Coventry a 3-2 victory

ow left: Who won the Cup?
e Sky Blues celebrate in
le as they parade their first
r major trophy. . .and
at a way to get it

Above: Italy bound Ian Rush
gives Liverpool the lead in the
Littlewoods Cup final. . .but
he who scores first does not
ALWAYS win!

Left: For the day belongs to
cheeky Charlie Nicholas. The
idol of the North Bank scores
twice to give Arsenal the
trophy. . .but no kisses for
Charlie. . .just a stranglehold
from Highbury team-mate
Tony Adams

ft: What a start for Graeme
uness and Rangers. They win
e Skol Cup 2-1 beating Celtic in
e Final. . .and didn't Ted
cMinn, Ally McCoist and Terry
tcher celebrate!

low left: Dundee United beat
rcelona en route to the UEFA
p Final. . .but Gothenburg are
t too good. United lose their
cond major final in five days

ght: Iain Ferguson wheels away
enjoy the moment which took
e Scottish Cup to Love Street.
s extra-time goal for St Mirren
ralds a dismal end to the season
gallant Dundee United.

low: Big Terry makes his
rk. England's captain scores
e goal which gives Rangers a
draw at Aberdeen and
nches their first Premier
ague title in nine years

Top: After Mexico – West Germany? Gary Lineker keeps up his fantastic scoring rate with a beauty against Northern Ireland in England's 3-0 European Championship win at Wembley

Above: Going out? Mark Lawrenson scores the goal which gives the Republic of Ireland a 1-0 win at Hampden and ends Scotland's hopes of making the European Championship finals

So look out for these two fiery Welshmen. I reckon they'll have them singing in the valleys for years to come.

Another youngster in the same mould is John Sheridan of Leeds United, already a regular in the Eire squad. Sheridan is a strong-running, highly skilled midfielder and, according to my old mate Maurice Setters, the former Manchester United skipper who is now assistant manager to Jack Charlton with the Republic, John has all the qualities to go right to the top in British football.

From what I've seen of John I wouldn't disagree with that. Last year he made tremendous progress, becoming a key man in Leeds United's dual bid for FA Cup and promotion glory. His urgent, clever midfield probings helped Leeds to an FA Cup semi-final and to come within minutes of promotion to the First Division – only late goals in extra time by Charlton prevented them going up.

People are already comparing John to another famous Leeds and Republic midfielder – the ultra-talented Johnny Giles – but this is unfair at this stage of his career. It should be remembered that it took Gilesy some time to establish himself as one of our finest midfield maestros. In fact, the little fellow started life on the right wing. It was only later that he settled into his little general's role alongside Sheridan's guiding light Billy Bremner. However, like Giles, John Sheridan is marvellously talented. His distribution is good with either foot and like Giles his forté is gathering the ball in midfield and bringing his forwards into play with cunning little chips and one–twos which cause havoc in any defence.

He can shoot as well. Young John loves nothing better than taking the responsibility of free kicks on the edge of the box and ITV viewers will remember his brilliantly taken free-kick goal against Charlton in the final play-off match. The goal put Leeds ahead in extra time, but, sadly for Leeds, it was not enough as Peter Shirtliff scored twice to deny Sheridan his night of glory.

Billy Bremner, I know, thinks highly of his protégé and his only problem will be holding on to him now that United have not been promoted. Already the big clubs are gathering to monitor Sheridan's outstanding talents. I think it's inevitable that John will move on, but he will be a player to watch and enjoy at top level in the seasons to come, so put the name John Sheridan in your notebook.... No matter whom he plays for he will be a force to be reckoned with.

One of the biggest football stages in Britain for any youngster to aspire to is that of St James's Park in Newcastle. There are no more fervent fans than the Newcastle United supporters and no better judges of players. Once a Geordie hero, always a Geordie hero, like Jackie Milburn, Malcolm Macdonald, Kevin Keegan and Peter Beardsley. Mind you, they had to produce the goods.

When Magpie supporters start to talk of 'Wor Paul' you can be sure that a new hero has been found ... and already United fans are predicting big things for Paul Gascoigne. And I'm with them all the way. Gascoigne was one of the finds last season, as he grew up under the threat of relegation alongside such hardened campaigners as Peter Beardsley and Paul Goddard. At the end of a gruelling season Gascoigne has matured into a player of quality and promise, already marked down in the Bobby Robson notebook as one for the future.

Gascoigne made his debut for England's Under-21s in the European tournament in

Franz the Forest flier showed most First Division full-backs a clean pair of heels last season

football field. In the days when Second Division football beckoned, the lad showed maturity beyond his years by covering every inch of St James's (and every other pitch). One moment he was back in defence helping to soak up the pressure, the next haring up field applying pressure of his own in a bid to push his forwards into goalscoring positions in the opposition penalty area.

Paul is not just a willing workhorse. He has excellent ball control at speed and is a fine passer of the ball. And like Robbo he can tackle like a tank. Look for him appearing in a few more Under-21 teams. He may need a little time, but he is exactly the type of player every good team needs. A whole-hearted aggressive competitor who just doesn't know when he's beaten: a true Geordie hero in the making if ever I saw one.

Where have all the wingers gone? That's been the cry from many fans as the tactical systems have taken over in recent years. It's true that the days when every kid wanted the number seven shirt above all others seem to have gone. But the memory of such as Tom Finney, Stanley Matthews, George Best, Cliff Jones, Eddie Gray, Willie Henderson, Jimmy Johnstone and others lingers on – not least in the minds of managers who used to play against them – and suddenly wingers are back in fashion.

One possible star of the future who caught my eye last season was little Franz Carr, the right-wing star of Nottingham Forest. At times last season there was more in the newspapers about Cloughie's famous fight with Franz's taxi-driver dad over the youngster's new contract than about young Carr's talent. But happily for all concerned, the situation was resolved and hopefully Franz will now be allowed to

France last summer and immediately made his presence felt. A player in the Bryan Robson mould, he is a powerfully built young man who has an immense capacity for midfield work. I watched him on several occasions last season and never failed to be impressed by his selfless non-stop running for United.

Described by England Under-21 boss Dave Sexton as a 'box-to-box' player, Paul, like Bryan Robson, is a workaholic on the get on with his career. And a fine career surely awaits if he buckles down to the job. Certainly for me, and I'm sure for thousands of fans, there is no better sight in football than a winger in full flight causing devastation and chaos in opposing defences. Flying Franz can certainly do that. His turn of speed is absolutely devastating. Put a ball before him and he can leave a full back stranded from a standing start. I well

Nigel Clough is heading for the heights – just like his Forest manager, otherwise known as Dad

remember a murky night at the City Ground when Brighton were torn to ribbons by pace which reminded me of my old Liverpool team-mate, Peter Thompson and Greavsie's great Spurs mate, Cliff Jones, the Welsh wizard.

If Franz has a fault it is that his finishing cross often leaves much to be desired. I know it is something Cloughie will sort out in time but how frustrating it is to see Franz destroy a full back only to ship a cross into a sea of legs in the penalty area rather than float it to young Cloughie and others gathering at the far post. Still, the boy has talent and, already a fixture in Robson's Under-21 squads, he just needs to sharpen his finishing act to blast his way into the full squad.

While I'm on about Forest, what about young Nigel himself? Surely he, too is a player who will give Forest fans pleasure for years to come. To my mind, he is a highly skilled young player with much vision. He has had two excellent debut seasons with Forest, and it must be difficult when your father is manager. After all, knowing Cloughie senior, he would not choose his own son unless he was absolutely sure he was better than anyone else in that position.

People often ask how he compares with his father. Well, the truth is he does have his father's eye for a chance, but I see him as less dynamic than his dad though with a fine touch around the box. Bobby Robson I know has been keeping close tabs on Nigel's progress. ... It might not be too long before he, too, gains that coveted full England cap.

These then are my 12 tips for the future. There are many more great kids in the pipeline and some are already making their mark in the new season.

The future looks bright.

4

Confessions of a Cup Final Commentator

Brian Moore

Brian Moore has been ITV's 'Mr Football' for almost 20 years. A self-confessed football enthusiast, Brian's face and voice are known to millions of soccer fans and throughout the world he is recognized as one of the most knowledgeable presenters and commentators in the business. Brian admits to a special love for FA Cup Finals (he has now covered 19 for ITV) and in this special article he remembers the early days that stimulated his interest and the magic moments which he has managed to portray to millions.

In one of my first Cup Finals as a radio reporter, Jimmy Greaves scored a typically cheeky goal for Spurs; in one of my first as a radio commentator, Ian St John scored the winner for Liverpool. So you see, I go back quite a long way!

Jimmy, of course, was the Mr Twinkle-toes in a Tottenham side that in 1962 beat Burnley 3-1; Ian was, I always felt, the more fearsome character with a keen competitive edge to match his talent. It was his superb finishing – a slick readjustment to meet a low cross with a triumphant header – that won the 1965 Final against Leeds. The winning partnership of Saint and Greavsie was still nearly 20 years distant!

But my Cup Final memories go back much further. As a dreamy country bumpkin, I remember well listening to the 1946 Cup Final between Derby County and Charlton on our big brown bakelite HMV radio. I was so naive that I couldn't understand the commentator when he talked of thousands of fans on the terraces. To my unworldly mind, a terrace was something you had at the back of the house, like a patio – that shows you how far removed I was from the world of professional football. I mention it now because then, of course, there was no football on TV. A few flashes on the cinema newsreel perhaps, but nothing else. Except that I remember I used to cycle to the next village every Sunday morning just to get a copy of the long-since defunct *Sunday Graphic* because they always had a back-page spread of football pictures.

Derby County won that year; Chris Duffy won the 1947 Final for Charlton and set a new fashion, I remember, by celebrating his goal with a joyous run back to the half-way line. The papers were full of it; now that sort of scene is commonplace; before Duffy, a handshake would usually suffice!

Then we come to the first Final I ever saw. The whole family piled into my Gran's cottage overlooking the village green while Grandad turned on the new TV set: a 9-inch screen set into a huge cabinet; a black and

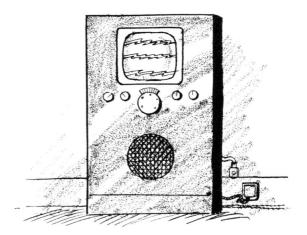

white picture, of course, and coverage, I'm sure, not nearly as sophisticated as we have today.

There were no slow-motion replays, no cameras behind the goal, no interviews before or after the game; no forties-style Saint and Greavsie; no studio guests. But for me it was my first sight of paradise: Wembley. As I remember, the sun was shining and the game was superb. Manchester United 4 Blackpool 2. Jimmy Delaney, Johnny Carey, Arthur Rowley in United's side; Stanley Matthews, Stanley Mortensen, Harry Johnston in Blackpool's. Those *Sunday Graphic* pictures had come to life. It was, I reckon, among the four best Finals since the war, to be ranked alongside the famous Matthews Final of 1953; the remarkable comeback by Everton against Sheffield Wednesday in 1966; and Coventry's supreme effort of such recent memory.

Little did I imagine as I sat there at the feet of various aunts and uncles that I would be privileged one day to help bring that sort of excitement to so many similar front rooms – and to have the great good fortune to go on doing so for 20 years and more. Dreams do sometimes come true.

Now, what about Mooro's memories then? The next few Finals were sketchy affairs for me – listened to in cricket pavilions on schoolboy Saturday afternoons and interrupted by National Service, so that I really only surfaced again in time for that brilliant Stanley Matthews Final for Blackpool against Bolton in 1953.

Everyone – outside Bolton that is – wanted Matthews and Blackpool to win. But with Bolton leading 3–1 and time fast running out in the second half, it seemed we would all be disappointed. It's history now that Stan weaved a special miracle down

Grand Stan finish ... Stanley Matthews (being chaired off, right) finally gets the Cup in his grasp after Blackpool's 4–3 win over Bolton

that right flank in front of the royal box and that Mortensen and finally Perry found a way past Bolton 'keeper Hanson – heavy polo-necked jersey and all on this scorching day – to make it 4–3 and send us running out into the village street like pools winners.

In the fifties I remember Ronnie Allen scoring a crucial penalty in 1954 for West Bromwich Albion against Preston and the picture next day of the Albion 'keeper Sanders clutching his goalpost, too nervous to watch. Then Bert Trautmann – the ex-German paratrooper, the newspapers called him – breaking his neck, or at least a bone in it, while keeping goal for Manchester City against Birmingham in the 1956 Final – City still won 3–1. And the next year, troubles for another goalkeeper as Manchester United's Ray Wood was charged ferociously by Aston Villa's Peter McParland.... Ray had to go off and as there were no substitutes in those days, Jackie Blanchflower took his place. United's 10 men were beaten 2–1.

These are random thoughts as we go into the sixties when Spurs won the Cup in 1961 and 1962 – there were times when they produced the most delightful and entertaining football I've ever seen. And it was effective, too. Just as with Liverpool for a spell in the early 1980s, you never felt they were going to lose. Spurs first beat Leicester, then Burnley.

By now I was a reporter with BBC radio and one of my Cup Final jobs was to get into the dressing rooms afterwards for the interviews. I don't remember it, but it was here that I might well have had my first professional encounter with J. Greaves, Esq.

We move on to 1964 and the West Ham–Preston Final was memorable for

Down not out … 'keeper Bert Trautmann treated for a neck that turned out to be broken before helping Manchester City lift the Cup

two things. West Ham won it with a last-minute goal from Ronnie Boyce – he told me just a few months ago that a devoted West Ham lady fan painted a picture of that moment and presented him with it: it still hangs in pride of place in the Boyce hallway. The second incident that jerks the memory back some 23 years is that Preston chose a 17-year-old as one of their wing halves. He was Howard Kendall. His first Wembley experience was boxed in by disappointment – but he's more than made up for that in recent years as the illustrious manager of Everton.

How did his nerves stand all the pressure? 'Not too badly,' says Howard:

I was only selected on the Wednesday before the match and I think that helped me. Remember in those days there was something like a six-week build-up between the semi-final and the Final and I was not involved in that at all. I did not expect to play – and when I got the nod there was no time to get nervous or up-tight. But it was still a massive disappointment, of course, when we lost.

As I've said, I remember the Saint winning a match in thrilling style for Liverpool in 1965 against Leeds, but a year later it was Everton's turn in a truly great game that perhaps never had quite the acclaim it deserves because it fell in the same year – 1966 – as another momentous football occasion at Wembley.

Sheffield Wednesday were two goals up, could have been more and were coasting. But Everton struck back at them and won 3–2. The Merseyside hero was a Cornishman whose name nobody quite knew how to pronounce: Mike Trebilcock. But was it Trebil*coe* or Trebil*cock*? Cockburns have made a fortune in port over just such a confusion! Mike scored twice, Derek Temple got one – there have been few Cup Final comebacks to match it. And as I reached the tunnel afterwards the Wednesday players were still in tears!

My first TV commentary was on the 1969 Final between Manchester City and Leicester. There wasn't very much special about my work and, to be honest, there wasn't very much special about the game either. Neil Young scored the only goal for Manchester City on an afternoon when the rivalry between ITV and BBC was even more fierce than between the competing teams.

Both TV teams were battling for the larger slice of the audience and pulled some crazy tricks to try to get the upper hand. For example, we had got hold of three or four Manchester City track suits to enable our crew to get to places where normally only players could go and so get the latest news. The BBC responded with a reporter hidden under a carpet, would you believe, in front of the team benches for that edge in manager interviews while the game was going on; and all around there were shabby scenes as both sides physically struggled to get key players in front of the cameras!

The TV companies and the FA realized this could not go on. And they were right. Indeed, when we look back now from a calmer, more dignified portrayal of football's greatest day, it's just amazing that it ever happened at all.

Chelsea won a fabulous replay against Leeds United in 1970 – played at Old Trafford in the days before everything started and finished at Wembley. The long throw was a new weapon in those days and nobody then – or since – could hurl it further than Chelsea's Ian Hutchinson. He found the head of David Webb and Leeds were beaten. But they were to return.

Not in the following year – 1971 – however, because this was the year of Arsenal's double. Bertie Mee's men held off Leeds for the First Division Championship and slipped skilfully past Liverpool for the Cup.

This was the final in which, for the first time, television was able to alter the official records. Liverpool were leading by a Steve Heighway goal when George Graham, their present manager, struck the Arsenal equalizer. Or so we thought. The camera surely could not lie. Except that the one placed behind the goal told quite a different story and was picked up by a backroom worker at London Weekend Television an hour before we went on air that night with a programme of Cup Final highlights.

The film showed that a shot by Arsenal's Eddie Kelly had at no point ever made contact with George Graham. That night we put the record straight – look in any reference book now and you'll find the scorer of Arsenal's first goal was Mr Kelly. One up to TV.

It was a wonderful game and, says Arsenal skipper Frank McLintock, an exhausting one:

By George ... Arsenal clinch the League and Cup double in 1971 as Charlie George's right hook floors Liverpool in the final

We had won the championship at Tottenham on the Monday and I got the Footballer of the Year Award on the Thursday and then we had to play Liverpool who were regarded as the fittest team in the land.

It went to extra time and, quite honestly, after it all I would like to have felt like the supporters felt. They looked overjoyed – I was just knackered! I did not feel the way I thought I was going to feel when we had a chance of doing the double. It was even a bit of an anti-climax. Even to this day it has always been a slight anti-climax and a puzzlement to me. I have always felt that one day it would sink in – but it never has.

Ray Clemence was the 22-year-old Liverpool 'keeper that day:

I thought I was in control of everything until I actually walked up the tunnel into the arena and the bright sunshine and the noise hit me. I froze completely and did not play that day to my true potential.

But I have to admit that the strike for the Arsenal winner by Charlie George was a great one. But what most people didn't realize – and probably still don't when they watch it on TV – is that it was actually deflected a little off Larry Lloyd's toe. It's always nice to think that had it not been deflected I might have got a touch to it.

Ray, also, would return to Wembley.

In 1973 we had what was a commentator's dream. Underdogs Sunderland were languishing near the foot of the Second Division, with apparently no chance against the Leeds machine that were Wembley's hottest favourites. We used to do a programme on the eve of the Cup Final called *Who'll Win The Cup?* consisting of studio experts, marks for attack, defence, creativity, etc., and a final verdict. Predictably Leeds won it hands-down. However, Sunderland won the game that mattered.

What memories that game inspired. Ian Porterfield's goal … Jim Montgomery's amazing series of saves in the second half … Sunderland manager Bob Stokoe's 50-yard run from the bench on the final whistle to seek out and hug his match-winning goalkeeper. Says Bob Stokoe now:

I think we are talking about one of the best Cup Finals in the last 20 years. My run to goalkeeper Jim? Well, something at the back of my mind reminded me of a save he had made at Notts County that got us a replay in an earlier round; he made a tremendous save at a critical

moment in the semi-final against Arsenal and I actually believe that at the end of the day he was the main reason we won the Cup.

It is something you never forget. I have a photograph of that save above my fireplace at home and sometimes when I look at it I even think the ball had gone over the line. Thank goodness it didn't! If ever a save won a Cup Final this was it.

My old chum Mike Channon has a saying: 'Live every day as your last. One of these days you'll be right.' He lived the day of the 1976 Final like no other – for Southampton, like Sunderland, the underdogs – now against mighty Manchester United. And Southampton won it 1–0. Says Mike:

All I remember was thinking that this will probably be the biggest occasion I'm going to

Sunderland in wonderland … match-winner Ian Porterfield (left) celebrates the shock defeat of then-mighty Leeds with Dennis Tueart

get in my life. I am not going to be beaten here – that is number one. And then Bobby Stokes scored our crucial goal. At last we put three passes together and with seven minutes left Stokesie hit it – not very well as it happens – but it went in and that's what mattered.

And Mike, I remember, had his testimonial game at the Dell two nights later. It must be one of the very few such games that became a sell-out. He always was a lucky so-and-so!

The mind skips on – to a victory for still unfashionable Ipswich over Arsenal in 1978 with a solitary goal by Roger Osborne. Bobby Robson was the Ipswich manager then and he says there could not have been a more popular match winner or a more deserved team of winners. 'We had a little vote in the dressing room before the game,' Bobby reveals 'and we asked who would we each like to see score the Ipswich winner. Everybody said the local lad Roger Osborne. And after the final whistle he was so overcome by the occasion we actually had to carry him off. He had gone – not with the physical effort – just the emotion.'

Then on to that incredible finish in 1979 – Arsenal two up against Manchester United and coasting near to the end of the second half. It hadn't been a very good game – but we had no idea as the minutes dragged on what was still in store. First Gordon McQueen and then Sammy McIlroy scored for United ... the balance of power in these last dramatic minutes would surely swing United's way. But no – Liam Brady was at the forefront again for Arsenal ... a chip in from the left ... Alan Sunderland's shot reaches the back of the net and Wembley can look back on another dramatic climax.

We nearly had another one in 1983 when Manchester United were overwhelming favourites to beat Brighton – Jimmy

Melia's dancing shoes notwithstanding. Yet with the score at 2–2 and with the last minutes of extra time already well advanced, Brighton's Michael Robinson surges up the left, his pass to Gordon Smith is perfect, only the goalkeeper to beat – except that Gary Bailey smothers the shot superbly. Was it a glaring miss? Was it an astounding and timely save? The arguments will never end. There was no argument about the replay. United won it 4–0.

United also won amidst controversy in 1985 when Kevin Moran was sent off – and was refused his medal from the royal box – but 10 men and a moment of inspiration from Norman Whiteside were enough to beat Everton. Said United's manager Ron Atkinson:

The funny thing is that we were playing Everton, the champions, and winners of the European Cup Winners' Cup and probably the best team in Europe at this time with only 10 men and yet I had the feeling that we could still do it.

I remember sitting on the bench with Kevin Moran and Arthur Albiston, who had just come off, and everybody was saying, 'If we can only hold on and have another crack at them on Wednesday.' I told them we'd beat them today. I just had the feeling that we were starting to grow even with 10 men and, as it worked out, Norman gave us all the greatest day and night of our lives.

That had been Everton's second successive Cup Final appearance. The previous year they had begun their fabulous comeback under Howard Kendall, climaxing an amazing year by playing Watford at Wembley. On that occasion they won 2–0 and again there had been controversy ... did Andy Gray foul Steve Sherwood before scoring the clinching second goal? Personally I don't think so, although some referees might have given the 'keeper the benefit of the doubt.

The Blues were back again in season 1985-6 to record three successive FA Cup Final appearances – a tremendous feat. This time it was the first-ever Merseyside Cup Final with Everton against their old rivals Liverpool, who were going for the double, having just pipped their local rivals for the Championship.

It was to be an amazing match. Kenny Dalglish was to be the first-ever player–manager to lead his team out at Wembley. Surely the double could not be achieved. It certainly didn't seem like it as Everton outplayed Dalglish's men in the first half, a goal from Barcelona-bound Gary Lineker putting the Blues in front.

I well remember young full back Jim

Beglin and Bruce Grobbelaar at one stage almost coming to blows, such was the pressure the Reds' defence was under. And it was Brucie who turned the tide for Liverpool. A fabulous stretching save touched over to prevent Liverpool going two goals down early in the second half gave his team fresh hope. Suddenly Everton were on the run and goals from the super-sharp Ian Rush (two) and Craig Johnston turned potential disaster into an historic League and Cup double win. Dalglish had done it all as player–manager in his first full season.

Which brings us to Coventry City. That amazing match against Tottenham is still a magical jumble of moments and memories that will only truly be unravelled in the years to come. I thought Spurs would skate

Quality of Mersey ... Liverpool player-boss Kenny Dalglish takes on Everton skipper Kevin Ratcliffe – and the Reds take the Cup

Finger on football's pulse ... Mooro at the Big Match *mike with the Saint taking a serious view of things*

it once they had got that early lead through Clive Allen, and the Coventry coach John Sillett admitted to me just the other day that his heart sank at that moment and he had a real fear that Coventry might be thrashed, that it was a day when Spurs would turn on their irresistible form.

Equally, once Coventry had drawn level the second time I couldn't see how Spurs would get their noses in front again. What exciting images that afternoon provides every time you think about it. The flying header by Keith Houchen – I don't suppose we have seen any better Cup Final goal; the agony of Gary Mabbutt when the ball skimmed off his knee and beyond Ray Clemence – has there been a more heart-breaking moment?

And what about John Sillett and George Curtis – like a couple of Edwardian Pierrots who had strayed from the end of the pier, larger than life, full of fun and good cheer and, as a football partnership, unbeatable on the day.

It was a Cup Final with a mystery to it as well. What about the confusion over Tottenham's shirts – some with advertising on the chests, some without. I don't suppose we shall ever get to the bottom of that one – or why it was so many trained observers in the press box and television commentary boxes failed to spot one of the biggest news stories of the day.

All I know is that every Cup Final I've been to has left me with something to treasure, something to regret and plenty to remember. And it's a long way back to Gran's front room and that 9-inch telly.

5

Winners and losers ... a pictorial record

In the following pages are chronicled the moments of glory, despair and drama which meant the difference between being a winner and a loser in season 1986–7.

Kop that ... Ian Rush acknowledges the cheers of his Anfield admirers after scoring in his farewell derby, a 3–1 defeat of Everton

First-class return ... Nigel Callaghan's delight says it all – Derby have booked a ticket back to the top flight and clinched the Second Division title

Right: *Arsenal take possession ... David O'Leary holds off Liverpool's Ian Rush (left) and Nigel Spackman and the Littlewoods Cup is Highbury-bound*

Left: England expects ... and Gary Lineker delivers his by-now customary goal, the first of two in a 3–0 defeat of Northern Ireland

Terry Butcher beats Alan McInally in a season when Rangers beat Celtic to the Skol Cup and Premier League

Above: Swindon's Tim Parkin (dark shirt) tussles with Trevor Aylott of Bournemouth

Right: Northampton's profilic striker Richard Hill – later bought by Watford

Below: Paul McStay gives Scotland a rare moment of success against Belgium

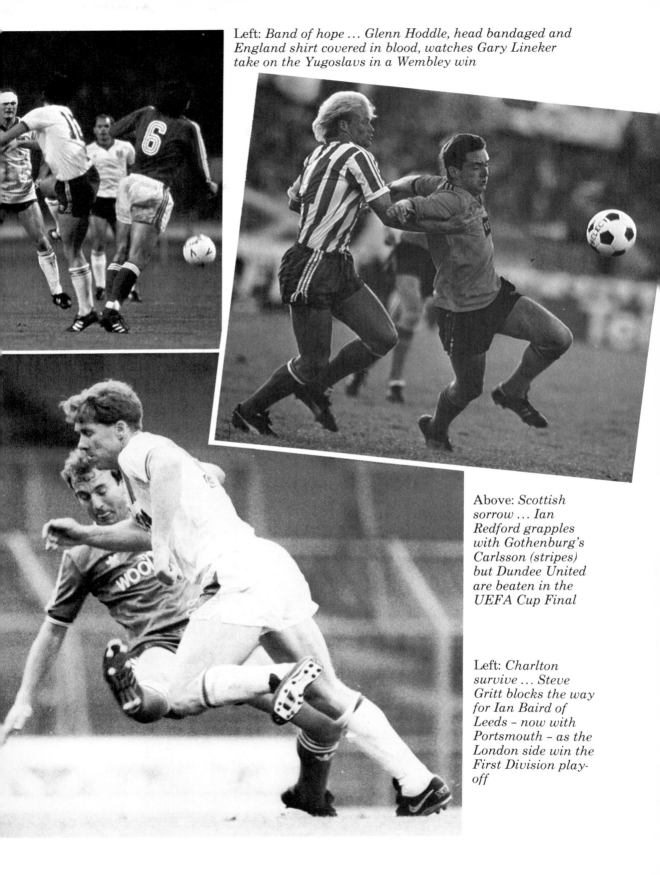

Left: *Band of hope ... Glenn Hoddle, head bandaged and England shirt covered in blood, watches Gary Lineker take on the Yugoslavs in a Wembley win*

Above: *Scottish sorrow ... Ian Redford grapples with Gothenburg's Carlsson (stripes) but Dundee United are beaten in the UEFA Cup Final*

Left: *Charlton survive ... Steve Gritt blocks the way for Ian Baird of Leeds – now with Portsmouth – as the London side win the First Division play-off*

Above: *Pride of Scotland ... Rangers take the Ibrox acclaim for winning the Scottish League, captain Terry Butcher holding the silverware*

Above: *Nuts in May ... Coventry players and fans go Cup crackers as Spurs rue Gary Mabbutt's own-goal misfortune*

Right: *Champions all ... Kevin Ratcliffe raise Football League championship trophy, but th Everton squad share in Goodison's glory*

Below: *Saints alive ... Iain Ferguson is about to crack St Mirren's Scottish Cup Final winner and break Dundee United hearts yet again*

Right: *Partners in climb ... Dave Watson rises above Craig Johnston, the story of the season really as Everton finished above Liverpool in another Mersey 1–2*

6

Our all-time greats

Ian and Jimmy

In this chapter Saint and Greavsie argue it out to select their dream team. Just who were the greatest? Ian and Jimmy call on their experience of playing with and against the maestros of world soccer plus their judgement as ITV panellists.

Greavsie: OK Saint, if we're going to pick our greatest team then we've got to decide on the formation – how about 5-4-3?

Saint: Don't think so Jimmy – that will give you 12 players. Now I know it seemed at times that the Spurs team you played in had 12 in it but it isn't allowed in FIFA circles.

Greavsie: Is it true FIFA stands for 'Fee for this and fee for that'?

Saint: No it isn't so behave yourself and let's get down to choosing our dream team, in a 4-3-3 formation, starting with the goalkeeper.

Greavsie: Well, we've narrowed it down to three – my old England team-mate Gordon Banks, the great Italian Dino Zoff and another team-mate of mine, Pat Jennings, formerly of Spurs and Northern Ireland … Now I know you fancy Zoff … tell me why.

Saint: Well, Dino would be my choice simply because I reckon he was the man

who held Italy together in that wonderful World Cup win in Spain in 1982.

Greavsie: What about Paolo Rossi then, I thought he did a fair job for the old spaghetti munchers.

Saint: Agreed, but Zoff was the skipper and he led by example. He was nearing 40 at the time and he was the man who always looked ice-cool in the midday sun of Spain. And if you remember, he held them together in the quarter-final tie with Brazil which they won. Some of his work was spectacular as the Brazilians tried to pull back their deficit. Anyway he was a marvellous 'keeper all his days. How many cups and leagues did he help Juventus to win over the years? I don't choose him just for his World Cup displays but also for the fact that he was a first-class, reliable goalie all his days.

Greavsie: Fair enough, but before we move on to Jennings – what about Banksie? Exactly the same could be said about him.

A first-class professional and totally relia-ble all his days. And remember those mar-vellous saves against Brazil in Mexico in 1970, including the one they call the grea-test … the reaction save from the Pele header?

Saint: I've nothing but respect for Gordon. God knows he foiled me and my Liverpool team-mates often enough over the years. But the question remains, was he the greatest ever? He certainly was in the same class as Zoff but I don't know if he was any better. …

Greavsie: Well, strangely I don't rate Bank-sie as my best-ever keeper – although that he was world-class there is no doubt.

Saint: OK then – convince me.

Greavsie: Well, my tip for the top would be Jennings. For not only did Pat do the business in the hardest League in the world for over 20 years, he also starred in a Northern Ireland side which to be honest was never of the highest calibre.

Saint: There's an argument that that has got to be a help to a 'keeper.

Greavsie: I've heard that one but it's a load of tosh. If you've got a good defence in front of you then you've got to have a better record as a 'keeper in the long run. The point is big Pat did it when the Irish were going through spells when there were no Blanchflowers, no McIlroys, no Bests giv-ing him a hand, and I think even your Ray Clemence man must admit the big fellow was superb both in the air and on the ground.

Saint: Well certainly I'll give you that. Many a game against Liverpool he saved for your Spurs lot – the Drury Lane Fan

Pat Jennings, the world's best 'keeper and most capped player, tips another England effort over the Northern Ireland bar to safety

Dancers, as my old boss Bill Shankly used to call you.

Greavsie: Don't get off the subject. I reckon Jennings was the best simply because he lasted so long at the highest level. After all, he finished his career only last year in Mexico against Brazil, with the honour of becoming the world's most capped goalkeeper. You can't argue with that.

Saint: That's true. OK I'll go along with you on that one. Big Pat gets the nomination ... so Pat Jennings is our goalkeeper.

Greavsie: Now we come to the tricky bits. Let's look at our defence – and the right back first, who do you fancy?

Saint: It's a position that I've felt over the years we Scots have had excellent players in. Remember Alex Hamilton in my day and in later years Danny McGrain?

Greavsie: I remember Hammy as a player all right. He was the cheekiest devil I've ever come across. When he came to London he felt he owned it. In fact, I felt he should speak with a Cockney accent. ... But you're right, he was a brilliant little full back. Quick in the tackle and ever ready to gallop upfield to urge on his forwards. He was as neat as a pin and certainly caused we English a bit of trouble.

Saint: I won't mention the 1963 2–1 match at Wembley in which Hammy starred then.

Greavsie: No ... and I won't mention the 9–3 game in which you lot didn't star. What was the gag at the time – nine past Haffey?

Saint: Back to business. Hammy was a class full back, and so I feel was Danny McGrain, who by the way, James, has just been freed by Celtic after 20 years.

Greavsie: Shows what you can do if you take care of yourself Saint. Just think I could still be playing if I'd looked after myself.

Saint: Yes, but could your team afford the wheelchair?

Greavsie: Cheek! But seriously, I know Danny was a class player but he had a gap in his career didn't he?

Saint: That's right – a mystery injury to his foot which followed his contracting diabetes in the 1974 World Cup. But it should be remembered he was one of the best overlapping full backs in the business. Scotland's success in the 1974 World Cup Finals was due in part to his being able to master some of the biggest names in the game and still have the energy to fly down the right wing to set up Dalglish and go up front.

Greavsie: McGrain was good, I'll give you that, but I reckon there can only be one choice for the right back spot – Carlos Alberto of Brazil.

Saint: Not a bad choice. Tell me more.

Greavsie: Well if you think back on the 1962, 1966 and 1970 World Cups, the Brazilians were the masters ... apart from a little team called England breaking the mould!

Saint: Don't digress Greavsie!

Greavsie: Sorry Saint ... I know you Scots enjoy being reminded of that. But really the Brazilians over that period were great and I would argue that Carlos Alberto set the pattern for all the attacking full backs who seemed to spring out of the woodwork in the sixties and seventies. The man was a genius. Always at hand when the opposition forwards were getting too close to their lousy goalkeeper, yet able to conjure a ball out of mid-air with both feet and suddenly turn defence into attack. Remember his forays into the Italian half in the 1970 World Cup Final in Mexico. He was the ideal full back, good in defence, great on the break and he could take a chance, too – remember his great goal in the Final?

Saint: OK Jim you've convinced me, Carlos Alberto for right back. That's 2–0 to you by the way. But what about our centre backs – do we go for two ball players, or a sweeper and a big stopper centre half like Jack Charlton?

Greavsie: Big Jack one of the world's best – don't make me laugh. Now if you're talking about hunting and fishing!

Saint: Only kidding. But seriously, I think one of your old England colleagues has got to come into consideration for one of the central positions.

Greavsie: I can't believe it ... a Jock admitting an Englishman's got talent.

Saint: Well, I don't think any Scot would disagree with this choice – hard though it might be to make. I plump for your old mucker Bobby Moore in the middle of our defence.

Greavsie: That's hard to believe. What was it your Tartan Army used to sing – 'Bobby Moore superstar ... walks like a woman and wears a bra!'

Saint: That's true but they did appreciate he could play. We always have appreciated good players – even you were thought to have talent.

Greavsie: I wish they had told Alf Ramsey that.

Saint: Seriously, Bobby Moore was one of the great players of his time. The man oozed class and leadership qualities. He was brave, quick and superbly balanced. Moore, to my mind, was the man more than any other on the pitch who won England the World Cup. I know Geoff Hurst scored the hat-trick in the Final but over the Wembley matches it was Moore who stood out. The thing about Bobby – and I played against him many times – was that he always seemed to have room to manoeuvre, always had space to play. And he could read a game to perfection. He never looked hurried and was looked up to by his fellow pros. I'll never forget at the end of the game in Leon when Brazil had beaten England 1–0 in 1970 (the Banks save match) ... at the end of a marvellous game Pele sought out Bobby to swap jerseys with him. The great Brazilian recognized a fellow traveller in class.

Bobby Moore, pride of West Ham and inspirational skipper of England's World Cup-winning boys of '66

Greavsie: I couldn't have put it better myself Saint. Mooro's in our team. I reckon that's worth a couple of pints of lager for you from the old boy – he does like a drop you know.

Saint: I've learned that to my cost over the years. But now we need someone alongside Bobby in the middle. Who do you suggest – big John Charles perhaps?

Greavsie: Or we could have Rattin, the giant Argentinian who was sent off against us in 1966. He was some player.

Saint: He was also, according to your old guv'nor Alf Ramsey, one of the 'animals'. We want a clean outfit Greavsie ... think again.

Greavsie: Well, assuming we're going for two great footballers in the middle how about the Kaiser? Franz Beckenbauer of West Germany – the most cultured player I've ever seen at centre back?

Saint: Won't he be too much like Mooro?

Greavsie: I don't think so. Both were superb footballers and had great vision. If either made a mistake then the other would cover up. I think they would make a great partnership. I've been a fan of Beckenbauer's ever since he appeared as a teenager in the 1966 World Cup Final against England at Wembley. You talk about Bobby always having room to play ... well if we're being truthful Franz always seemed to have even more space when he was on the ball. I remember him in the match against England in the 1970 World Cup quarter-finals in Mexico. England were two goals up but Beckenbauer kept urging on his men and eventually after Alf Ramsey made his one and only blunder as England team manager by pulling off Bobby Charlton, he got

Franz 'Kaiser' Beckenbauer, West German captain with Bobby Moore-style coolness in the heat of a battle

his team to believe in themselves. The rest is history – England lost 3–2 and the Kaiser led his troops into the semis.

And it was the same in West Germany in 1974. I don't think West Germany were the best team in the tournament – Holland were by far the better outfit – but Beckenbauer kept prompting, kept them going by example and eventually they beat the Dutch in the Final (albeit a bit fortunately). No, I reckon Moore and Beckenbauer would give us class in the middle of the defence. One could play off the other and either would be capable of launching an attack whenever necessary. So it's Kaiser Franz for me, Saint.

Saint: I'll go along with that Jimmy. Franz was a topper … and before you even begin to nominate a left back I'll nominate one for you - Ray Wilson your old England colleague.

Greavsie: You've just chosen two Englishmen in succession Saint - you'll be drummed out of the clans for that.

Saint: Well, credit where credit's due. Ray was one of the greatest full backs I've ever seen in my life, and while others such as Gentile of Italy spring to mind, I think Ray wins it for his sheer consistency of performance.

Greavsie: I couldn't agree more, Saint. You know it's been mentioned in the book already, but I only saw him make one mistake in all his days as an England full back - the faulty back header to Gordon Banks which allowed Haller to score for West Germany in the 1966 World Cup Final.

Saint: I know, and it's amazing how after all the great years that's the one moment people remind Ray of. But he was a great

full back. He played against me often for Everton in the Merseyside derby matches and his duels with Peter Thompson were something to behold.

Like all good full backs he would jockey a player out to the touchline and then when the winger got frustrated he was in like a whippet to steal the ball and charge upfield. A great defender and working as an undertaker now you know, Greavsie.

Greavsie: Still laying them in the aisles then, Saint?

Saint: Behave yourself Jimmy. Now we've got our back four – Alberto (Brazil), Moore (England), Beckenbauer (West Germany) and Wilson (England). What about midfield?

Greavsie: The trouble is, Saint … where do you begin when you think of some of the great midfielders we've played with and against and watched? It's mouth-watering.

Saint: That's true Greavsie but let's get down to it. My two tips for the right midfield position are both Brazilians - the fabulous Didi and the marvellous Gerson.

Greavsie: Why them? I thought you were a Graeme Souness man?

Saint: Well, Souness was good in his time but I believe Didi and Gerson did almost as much for Brazilian World Cup winning teams as Pele himself. In fact, some of my earliest television highlights were of Didi's skills in Sweden in the 1958 World Cup – the one Pele was discovered in. I remember watching blurry pictures on an old black and white monitor and being spellbound at this amazing midfielder as he controlled the ball with either foot and brought his forwards into play with tantalizing little chips and through-balls. He was a wonderful player and, although that was probably the first World Cup to make an impact on television viewers, had he been playing today he would be lauded as the greatest.

Greavsie: He could play all right. I had the pleasure of playing against him in Chile in 1962 and the thing that struck me about him was that he always seemed to be on the ball. Everything revolved around him – including some fairly well-known Englishmen. He had us in such a spin in their 3–1 quarter-final win over us. But what about Gerson?

Saint: Well he, too, was a superb right-fielded player, although not in the same style as Didi, who was really an outright attacking wing half as we knew them in those days.

Dave Mackay, (pictured in his Derby days) whose fearless tackles made the Saint and Greavsie glad to be team-mates with Scotland and Spurs respectively

Gerson was a more thoughtful, less spectacular player but he, too, was an inspiration to Brazil when they won the World Cup in 1970. He had tremendous vision allied to an all-action style and with that bit of extra ball control which all Brazilians seem to have. He was a true great.

Greavsie: He was, too, but I think I've got someone better than both who would always be in my team … and since you've been charitable enough to choose two Englishmen, you'll be happy to know that this one's a Scot – old lionheart himself, Dave Mackay.

Saint: A great player, but why him in preference to such as Didi and Gerson?

Greavsie: Well, I believe every great team needs a strong man – a player of fire and character who can drive them on to success when they are down – and Mackay was that kind of player. I can see him yet: that great barrel chest trapping a ball, letting it fall to his knee and then his foot, before pushing forward to launch another attack. And all the time he was urging players around him to great things. He led by example and was a natural leader of men. And he could tackle like a tank. I tell you if anyone went into a tackle with Mackay they had to mean it. There was no flinching from Dave – even after two broken legs. No, I realize that the likes of Didi and Gerson perhaps had more natural skills than Dave, but they didn't have his bottle or his aggression. He was a fighter and he made his team fight all the way to the final whistle. He would have to be in my team of teams, Saint.

Saint: I'm with you, Greavsie – particularly when I think of what a morale booster he was off the park as well. I remember his

Diego Maradona, showing his fantastic balance, control and swerve for Argentina ... and without using his hands!

favourite trick: tearing up fellow Scots' complimentary tickets before an international. That always got a laugh. Mind you, it stopped abruptly when the late John White turned the tables on him by switching Dave's own tickets. With the entire Scots pool in stitches Dave ripped up his own briefs ... strange he never tried that one again! But yes, Greavsie, Mackay gets my vote too. What about the other two midfield positions?

Greavsie: This is where it gets tricky, Saint. Let's think who we've got to choose from – Michel Platini of France, Omar Sivori of Argentina, George Best of Northern Ireland, Jim Baxter of your lot, Johnny Haynes, whom I suppose would be looked on as a midfielder nowadays, Ossie Ardiles, Rivelino of Brazil – they could all play a bit you know.

Saint: And let's give a hand for the man himself, Diego Maradona.

Greavsie: Leave it out Saint, although I admit you've got a point.

Saint: I'm sure I have Greavsie, and I reckon no world team can be without the greatest players in the world, and Diego is simply the best in the world. Let's face it, his first goal against England might have been a trifle suspicious but his second was a diamond.

Greavsie: Agreed, Saint – but would he fit in in midfield?

Omar Sivori, a great Argentinian from Greavsie's brief Italian sojourn who blazed the trail for Maradona and Co

Saint: I believe so, for he is at his best gathering the ball around the centre circle and charging off on those marvellously skilful runs. He really was sensational in the World Cup, and he is so strong that he is rarely knocked off a ball. His balance is superb and he reminded me of a little bull as he charged his way into opposing penalty areas. And when he gets there he is a lethal finisher … and let's face it, with Mackay backing him up he can freewheel upfield whenever he likes, knowing that the iron man is right behind him.

Greavsie: OK, it goes against the grain as an Englishman, but I'll give you Maradona if you go along with my choice for left midfield.

Saint: Don't tell me – Jim Baxter?

Greavsie: No, I've always been a big admirer of Baxter, but he didn't do it for long enough – as an Englishman I thank God for that – and while that left foot of his was magical I reckon Omar Sivori, the tricky little Argentinian who used to play for Juventus while I was with AC Milan in Italy, was one of the masters of the game.

He wasn't a big fellow but like Maradona he could twinkle his way past the greatest Italian defenders with ball control I've never seen the like of since. He was an aggressive little rascal, too. He was always in bother with the referees – mainly due to the hammering people tried to give him. But as the left-sided midfielder he had no equal as far as I'm concerned. The man was mystical the way he could ghost through a defence. He was a real will-o'-the-wisp and could sell a dummy as easy as pie. Sivori was a genius there's no doubt about that.

Saint: Fair enough, Jimmy – Mackay, Maradona and Sivori – not a bad midfield. But now for the front line, and there's one man we must get in, the great Alfredo di Stefano at centre forward.

Greavsie: I don't disagree with that one, Saint – he was certainly one of the best of all time.

Saint: The thing about Alfredo was his ability to lead a line as well as take a chance. Scots fans still rave about his performance in the famous match at Hampden in 1960 when Real Madrid beat Eintracht Frankfurt in what is widely recognized as the best European Cup Final ever. Di Stefano, aided and abetted by the great Ferenc Puskas and the flying winger Gento, scored three for Real that night and I don't think I've ever seen a better display by a centre forward. His pace was unreal as he turned the Eintracht defence, and his one–twos with Puskas were a joy to behold. And his finishing power was awesome. I was lucky enough to play alongside him in a special media match during the World Cup in Argentina – and even at over 50 he was still magic.

Greavsie: You must have been the only Scot to get a kick in Argentina, Saint! But no argument – di Stefano goes in at number nine. But now we come to the toughies. We're running out of places – only two left and still with the likes of Stan Matthews, Tom Finney, Pele, Johan Cruyff and George Best standing on the touchline.

But first things first. You've said that the greatest players of the era must go in, so Pele just cannot be left out.

Saint: I go along with that Jimmy, for I've rarely seen a more complete footballer than the great Brazilian.

Greavsie: Exactly, Saint. And like you, I remember sitting before a black and white telly watching Pele making a winning debut in the Brazil team which won the

Di Stefano, a centre-forward who combined great class and courage, scores for Real Madrid in the 7–3 crushing of Eintracht Frankfurt in the 1960 European Cup Final at Hampden

Above: *Pele, pictured as a 17-year-old wonderboy scoring Brazil's third in the 5–2 victory over Sweden in the 1958 World Cup Final*

Right: *George Best, wild-haired wing genius from Northern Ireland who was as strong as he was skilful*

1958 World Cup in Sweden. Mind you, I wasn't sitting for long – the kid's skills were so great he had me out of my chair every few minutes ... some kid!

But really the man was great for a long time. It was one of my big regrets that he was kicked out of the World Cup finals in England in 1966, for I'm sure had he survived the banditry that went on he would have guided Brazil to the Final to play England. The man had everything. A great physique, wonderful ball skills and that little bit of devilment every master of football has in his make-up. Who will ever forget the fantastic dummy against Uruguay and the lob from the half-way line against Czechoslovakia which just missed in the 1970 World Cup Finals. Those efforts were touched by greatness and his all-round skill and poise thrilled millions around the world, for luckily he was of the television era in world football. I doubt if there will ever be anyone as good again.

Saint: Pele it is on Alfredo's right-hand side then, Greavsie – but what about the left?

Greavsie: Well, we've a few promising lads left, Saint – Puskas, Rossi, Dalglish, Matthews, Finney, Cruyff, Cliff Jones, George Best, Denis Law.

Saint: And, I would suggest, one James Greaves, Esq. But since you're co-manager

of this team you're ruled out, Jim. But it's still a tough choice. Can you imagine an all-time great team without Matthews, Puskas, Finney and co?

Greavsie: I can't Saint, but we've only one place left, and the choice must be unanimous ... so who do you go for?

Saint: Bestie gets my vote Jim and I know that you are as big an admirer of the Irish fellow as I am.

Greavsie: That's right Ian, and with apologies to all the other greats we've mentioned, George is due his place. For in the sixties he was Britain's number one footballer – the first player ever to have pop star or TV star adulation. And it was thoroughly deserved. People say he peaked too early, that he got everything too quickly. That may be so, but he was in my opinion the greatest player ever to come out of these islands of ours.

I remember watching him as a kid outwitting the entire Spurs defence with that leggy catch-me-if-you-can style of his before slipping the ball through for the Lawman to score. Best had magic in his feet. And although frail and weak-looking, he always came out from jousts with the strongest tacklers with the ball at his feet. His ball control was fantastic and sometimes I was afraid our defenders would screw themselves into the ground the way he turned them inside out.

Saint: That's right Jimmy, our team were no mugs either and Tommy Smith was no respecter of reputations, but Tommy knew he had a handful when George was in opposition. And the lad could not only make goals, he could score them. Spectacular goals in which he would drag the ball across and through packed defences before popping in great goals. A wonderful player, and one who, had Northern Ireland been strong at the time, would have been up there on the world stage with the likes of Pele, Cruyff, Beckenbauer and the rest. Perhaps he did go out of the game early because of his problems, but I for one enjoyed his marvellous skills while they lasted.

Greavsie: Me too, Saint and perhaps those that criticize him should remember that few great players can explain their talent and fewer still can handle it. George was like his home country's favourite brew ... SHEER GENIUS.

Saint: So this is our team, Jimmy: Jennings (Northern Ireland); Alberto (Brazil), Moore (England), Beckenbauer (West Germany), Wilson (England); Mackay (Scotland), Maradona (Argentina), Sivori (Argentina); Pele (Brazil), di Stefano (Spain), Best (Northern Ireland) – not a bad eleven I reckon.

Greavsie: But let's cheat a little; let's play World Cup rules and name the five subs we've already agreed on: Zoff (Italy), Charles (Wales), Didi (Brazil), Matthews (England), Cruyff (Holland).

Saint: No modern-day players make it then, Jimmy?

Greavsie: No, Saint, although Bryan Robson and Kenny Dalglish came close.

Saint: Maybe it's us that's getting old, Greavsie?

Greavsie: Maybe so Saint, but I tell you what, I wouldn't half fancy our chances of making a few bob out of the lot we've picked down the Hackney Marshes on a Sunday!

Saint and Greavsie
AND THE TEMPLE OF GLOOM!

WRITTEN AND
ILLUSTRATED BY
BARRY ROBERTS

Look at that Saint! Dickie Davies has nicked all the parking spaces again.

We'll have to use the Producer's bike shed, Jim.

LONDON WEEKEND T.V. STUDIOS. THE SAINT AND GREAVSIE ARRIVE FOR WORK

DD 2

MEANWHILE, IN THE SPORTS OFFICE.

Here's a note from the Guv'nor. Urgent business come up, back in ten minutes

Maybe the coffee machine's broken down.

Get your feet off the desk and stand to attention, Greavsie! The P.M.'s on the line!

Could be about her hat trick.

Hello Guv. Just reading about the F.A. Cup being stolen. Funny old game ain't it!

Prime Minister speaking. You must find that F.A. Cup at all cost. Denis will be most upset if he's nothing to present at next week's final. He knows all about football of course... Despite watching your shows every week.

SPEED IS ESSENTIAL. SO A DICKIE DAVIES ROLLS ROYCE IS COMMANDEERED.

He'll never miss just one Roller, Jim. Wonder why the P.M. chose us for the job?

Probably a suicide mission. Like when they sent me up to interview the Accies.

F.A. HEADQUARTERS. SECRETARY, FRED POKER WAITS.

It was Hans Beckenflour. He knocked out the guard and made off with the cup.

Look Jim, a cigar. Beckenflour must have dropped it.

And there's only one place you can get these, Mr Poker. South America!

Let's hope we're not too late.

A SPECIALLY DIVERTED CONCORDE TAKES OFF WITH THE BOYS ON BOARD. HANS BECKENFLOUR, LOSING CAPTAIN IN THE 1966 WORLD CUP HAD ALWAYS SWORN REVENGE. SO THIS WAS IT. STEALING THE F.A. CUP A WEEK BEFORE THE FINAL.

Nice of old Brian Moore to lend us his private plane, Saint!

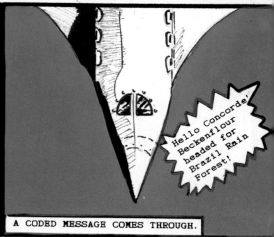

Hello Concorde. Beckenflour headed for Brazil Rain Forest!

A CODED MESSAGE COMES THROUGH.

GOD ACKO HOLDS COURT

The Saint and Greavsie require an audience, Sire.

I'm not surprised judging by that show of theirs!

Greetings Acko. We're looking for the F.A. Cup. Have you seen it?

Yeh. 1985. Beat Everton one nil in the final! Actually, I'm just about to have some lunch. Champagne and caviar. But I'm sure I can manage a cup of tea and a bun for you two.

THEY DECLINE SO ACKO TELLS ALL.

Beckenflour passed by two days ago. He carried the cup in a cloth bag. . even offered it to me! But I told him, no German's giving me the sack! So I've arranged someone to look after you. Tarzan of the Stretford End. The finest defender in the country.

BUT BECKENFLOUR IS READY.

If ze English vont ze cup zey vill 'ave to defeat ME first! But unlike '66, zer vill be no referee to 'elp!

ACKO'S DEFENDER APPROACHES.

Isn't he supposed to swing through trees?

Not with that bad shoulder of his!

Greetings. I am Tarzan of the Stretford End, here to defend you. Beckenflour has fled across the mighty river. Only one man can get us across. The Forest Keeper.

The keeper of the Forest, Jim. You don't think he means?

Nah. . couldn't be the same one, Saint. Besides, How would he recognise it? He's never SEEN the F.A. cup!

THEY REACH THE RIVER.

Stay where you are young man. I'll come over to your side.

Beckenflour sank all the boats so I'll carry you across.

Blimey Saint! It is him!

THE SAINT IS CARRIED OVER FIRST. THEN IT IS JIM'S TURN.

Time you lost a bit of weight, Jim.

It's all those long periods of inactivity that do it. Especially on Sporting Triangles

SAFELY ACROSS THE RIVER.

Thanks Forest man. Expertly done.

Plenty of practice young man. I've had the press on my back for years! But go careful. A deadly Marksman lies in wait, in the rushes.

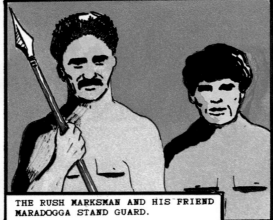

THE RUSH MARKSMAN AND HIS FRIEND MARADOGGA STAND GUARD.

BECKENFLOUR HAS TAKEN THE CUP INTO THE TEMPLE OF GLOOM, A DANGEROUS PLACE, ALMOST AS DANGEROUS AS LEEDS UNITED IN THE SIXTIES! WHEREIN LIES A CURSE CONDEMNING ANY TRESPASSER TO DEATH, OR EVEN MORE HORRIFYING, A SEASON TICKET FOR MANCHESTER CITY! OUR DYNAMIC DUO MUST ENTER!

THE SAINT DECIDES IT LOOKS DANGEROUS.

AA TEMPLE OF GLOOM

ENTRANCE

After fifteen years facing the likes of Norman Hunter not much frightens ME Saint

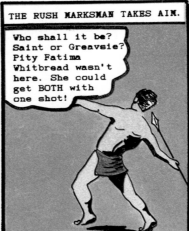

THE RUSH MARKSMAN TAKES AIM.

Who shall it be? Saint or Greavsie? Pity Fatima Whitbread wasn't here. She could get BOTH with one shot!

Where did that come from?

Probably a stray Uruguay supporter from the 86 World Cup!

THE CUP IS ON A PEDESTAL SURROUNDED BY CROCODILE INFESTED WATER!

THEY ENTER THE TEMPLE. GREAVSIE IS REMINDED OF HIS EARLY DAYS PLAYING FOR ALF RAMSEY.

Y'mean the long walk up the tunnel?

No, I mean everyone being kept in the dark. Listen! what's that rumbling?

SUDDENLY, A HUGE STONE FOOTBALL ROLLS TOWARDS THEM

I've heard of players chasing the ball but never this!

BECKENFLOUR'S PLAN RUNS TO SCHEDULE AS TWO ROBOTS APPROACH BEARING A STRIKING RESEMBLANCE TO OUR HEROES!

BUZZ BUZZ

SOMEONE MUST CROSS THE WATER BUT GREAVSIE SAYS HE CAN'T SWIM

Since when?

Since about two seconds ago! Now if you were Martin Tyler you'd be safe. Those are MAN eating crocs! But don't worry, Saint, wear this.

Even a CROCODILE wouldn't swallow that!

ACCIES FOR THE CUP!

THE SAINT REACHES THE CUP. UNKNOWN TO HIM, THE PEDESTAL IS BOOBY-TRAPPED

AS THE CUP IS LIFTED A STEEL CAGE FALLS FROM ABOVE.

CRASH

Look out!!

BECKENFLOUR APPEARS AND TELLS JIM OF HIS PLAN TO REPLACE OUR DUO WITH ROBOTS. NOT ONLY GAINING CONTROL OF THEIR SHOW BUT ALSO OF BRITISH FOOTBALL.

You've overlooked something. No one ever takes any notice of what we say!!!

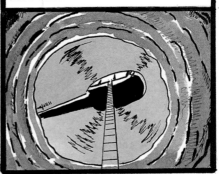

7

Have camera will travel

Jim Rosenthal, Martin Tyler,
Peter Brackley

Jim Rosenthal, Martin Tyler and Peter Brackley are the Three Musketeers of the *Saint and Greavsie* show on Saturday afternoons. Their motto is 'Have cameras will travel' as they travel the length and breadth of Britain to bring viewers the feature items they watch every Saturday lunchtime. This chapter brings the three together on a single theme – the perils of sports reporting.

———— Jim Rosenthal ————

Jim Rosenthal is one of television's most respected sports personalities, with an abundance of presentation and reporting experience behind him. Jim established himself as ITV's number one football reporter during the World Cup campaigns in Spain and Mexico and as an all-rounder he also presents athletics and boxing for the network.

A die-hard Oxford United fan, he learned his trade in radio, and his humour and hard-hitting style are reflected in this article in which he reminisces on some marvellous and hilarious moments . . . both on and off the football field.

We all know who the Saint and Greavsie played for, but what about the commentators? The Parrys, the Tylers, have they got a team? Do they know what they're talking about or do they just make it up as they go along?

It's my job here to tell you about our team. It may not be Tottenham and England or Liverpool and Scotland, but we do our best. The Commentators team has been going for around 15 years now and the first really unusual aspect is that BBC and ITV play

Jim Rosenthal

on the same side and occasionally manage to pass to one another as well!

Many have sipped briefly at the Commentators' wine glass and moved on. As the years have raced by and the grey hairs and pulled muscles increased, all of us have considered giving up and doing something more sensible. But we're still going … average age is now in the very late thirties … our reactions are getting slower and we have to lean more and more on our commentary skills to talk us through the 90 minutes.

John Motson, the BBC's top football commentator, is a founder member and one of the cornerstones of the side. He's a neat, precise and accurate midfield player or left back. Crunching tackles aren't his strong point, but he makes up for this with a shrewd positional sense and the lung power of a gazelle.

If he's that good why hasn't he played for England, I hear you ask. Several reasons

can be put forward in John's defence. He had to choose between playing and reporting when the North London giants were alerted to his promise some years back, and the demands of clawing his way up the ladder to *Match of the Day* meant he couldn't accept the offers.

You don't believe me? I can't say I blame you. But belief is what keeps us going. Somewhere inside of us we all think we should have played at the level that we talk about. Some of us are more deluded than others, but our team is often boosted by men who did it for real at the highest level until the years caught up with them.

Bobby Robson is one of these. The England manager, who did nothing towards lowering the average age of the team, played superbly in defence against Steve Cram's Athletes XI in Gateshead last year. I was managing the side that day which included Frank Bruno up front and Fish, the lead singer from the pop group Marillion. An interesting assortment!

'Bobby meet Fish – he's your left side midfield player,' I said. Now Fish is a daunting figure. More than 16 stones of Scottish power who had been talking match tactics deep into the early hours of the previous night. Shoulder-length hair, bleary eyed and struggling to find a suitable pair of shorts, it's fair to say that Fish was a far cry from Steve Hodge.

Mr Robson might not have been aware that the sight of Fish scouring the dressing room for kit would have caused a female riot at pop concerts all over the world. To him, Fish was on his side that morning and that was good enough.

Bobby Robson went on to take the Man of the Match award in a 5–5 draw and was very upset when we missed a great late chance to win. All right, it was Gateshead

Stadium and not the Aztec in Mexico City but it was a serious game and the outcome for a professional football man is all-important.

Frank Bruno scored that day with a very decent finish – shooting across the 'keeper from just inside the area. He could well have been a contender at football as well. There are two things I remember about big Frank: his pre-match threat to 'go out and kick some butt' and his apparent reluctance to head the ball after taking up some excellent positions at the far post – a strange contrast that from one of the bravest men around in British sport who's prepared to risk himself in the ring against the likes of Mike Tyson.

My ITV colleague Alan Parry is another regular. Right back is Alan's position and woe betide anyone who dares put on the number two shirt. Pat Rice of Arsenal and Northern Ireland stupidly assumed that he might be asked to don that number one day – after all, Pat has played there before. It made no difference – in the Commentators XI the number two shirt belongs to Parry and I get the feeling that if he ever quits we will follow the American tradition and retire the number as well!

Over the years we haven't always been popular with the refereeing fraternity, although we're all mellowing a bit now. I believe the tension and frustrations of the business we're all involved in used to boil over on the field and some officials seemed to take a special delight in having a go at the better-known 'faces' in the side.

Our stormiest matches seemed to take place when we went on tour. In Majorca, reinforced by the former Chelsea and Fulham striker Teddy Maybank, we needed a police escort away from a village in the hills after the referee decided to call the match off following an incident in which Frank Bruno's presence would have been decidedly handy.

In Florida the local official's interpretation of the rules was a very individual one and we had another stormy match which ended, in a raging thunderstorm, in a 5-4 victory. Peter Mellor, once an FA Cup Final 'keeper with Fulham, and Roger Hunt, a member of the 1966 World Cup winning side, were both fine tourists and both scored that day. Roger got the winner

and for him that saturated school pitch could have been Wembley in June 1966. He said that the feeling of winning any game is no different.

Martin Tyler is another regular in the line-up. He used to play for Corinthian Casuals in the Isthmian League and once lined up against the new Watford manager Dave Bassett. Martin takes his game very seriously and his aerial power has got us out of trouble many times. Speed over the ground isn't his strong point but next season, at some stage, I'm sure Martin will break out into a jog.

The 1987 version of the Commentators relies heavily on Gordon Riddick. Gordon played over 400 League games and had fallen out of love with football when we persuaded him to join us. Now he's a regular at centre half and also managed to achieve something he failed to do as a professional – namely a Wembley appearance in a charity match before the Freight Rover Trophy final in May.

Alongside Gordon, Steve Walford from BBC's *Match of the Day* team is another long-standing servant who could definitely have played at a higher level. We're boosted by young legs from the Old Reptonians – winners of the cherished public schools' football prize, the Arthur Dunn Cup, in 1987.

Roger Smith is the player-manager. Roger was on the Spurs books in the early sixties and was unlucky to be there at the same time as Jimmy Greaves. In fact, while Jimmy was terrifying First Division defences, Roger was top scorer in the Reserves. Without him the team would not exist. Every season Roger threatens to hang up his boots on the rusty nail for the last time but he keeps going, despite intense provocation, and so do we all.

Ron Atkinson has played for and against us. Once, when he was in the opposition, he poked his head round our dressing room door before the kick off and said: 'I see nothing here to worry us and no one who can possibly prevent me from being Man of the Match.' Whenever he played for us Ron insisted on one thing – he had to take all the free kicks. I'd spent my boyhood Saturdays watching The Tank, as he was known, run the midfield for Oxford United at the Manor. His commitment was total and he's the same now – the only trouble is that his free kicks haven't improved!

Steve Cram is a football nut who has suffered hugely at seeing his beloved Sunderland drop into the Third Division. Britain's highest-paid athlete gets £15,000 every time he sets foot on the track. Those long legs are worth a fortune but Steve plays football with absolutely no regard for his own safety. Those long legs go diving in for tackles or to try to get a scoring touch in the hurly-burly of the opposing penalty area.

Steve will go anywhere for a game. Once he flew down from Newcastle to London just to play for us against a schoolboy side who could not believe their eyes when Steve lined up against them very shortly after winning the gold medal at the European Championships 1500 metres.

What's Steve Cram the footballer like? Brave, decent control, good all-round ability and knowledge. Who knows what he might have done if only he had some pace!

Now the Saint has played for us occasionally but his appearances have been restricted by a dodgy ankle. We would all love to see more of him, but I get the impression that reducing his golf handicap is his priority these days.

A few years ago we played against a side that included Greavsie on Hackney Marshes in East London. The mud there has a cloying texture all of its own – I reckon you need a blowtorch to get it off. We detailed John Motson to do a man-to-man marking job on the great man. After all, Jimmy had gone at the game. He didn't look very fit and we all knew he hadn't exactly been looking after himself all that carefully. Hackney Marshes was hardly White Hart Lane or Wembley – why should Jimmy Greaves bother to put on any sort of performance here?

All good theories and all 100 per cent wrong. Jimmy was brilliant. He scored four in the first 25 minutes and his control and

finishing were absolutely deadly. At our half-time inquest we turned on poor John and asked him what was going on. 'I'm trying my best,' was the reply. Defenders and markers had said the same thing over the years, although not as politely as John,

after failing to stifle Jimmy's genius.

We Commentators will continue to try our best until the boots go on to that rusty nail for the last time. After all, as any former professional will tell you, there's nothing like playing the game. ...

Martin Tyler

Martin Tyler is one of television's best-known sports journalists. Martin has covered World Cups, European Championships and Olympics for ITV Sport as a commentator and is a regular reporter on *Saint and Greavsie.*

He is also one of the most prolific writers of football books – his *Boys of '66* is recognized as the 'bible' on England's winning World Cup campaign of 1966. A football fanatic with a wealth of experience behind him, in this feature he gives his list of dos and don'ts for prospective *Saint and Greavsie* reporters.

Martin Tyler

I'm sure that many of our younger viewers would like to become a reporter on the *Saint and Greavsie* programme so I thought I'd take the next few lines to pass on a few tips for the job. If you can master the DOS and DON'TS laid down by our revered producer Bob Patience, you'll be on course to become the Rosenthal, Brackley, Welsby or Tyler of the future.

DO have a working knowledge of the highways and byways of the Football League locations. The producer, a recent migrant from Glasgow, is likely to think you can pop from Manchester to Middlesbrough in half an hour and you must be able to dissuade him from such assignments.

DON'T interview Wimbledon players at their exotic pre-Cup tie headquarters wearing clothes that might shrink should you be foolish enough to try to capture the atmosphere of the location in a pool-side interview!

DO also beware of visits to Liverpool where the players take a particularly playful view of interviews. When I was the reporter on their team coach on the way to the 1986 FA Cup Final, there was an attempt – happily unsuccessful – to remove my trousers while we were on the air live.

DON'T, however, be lured by mischievous Tottenham stars into addressing Osvaldo Ardiles as 'Gandhi' during a live transmission. Sorry, Ossie, for bringing it up on the way to Wembley 1987. Clearly you were not amused.

Staying with Spurs, DO take a reference book with you to interview Clive Allen, or indeed any record-breaking goalscorer.

But if the record to be broken belongs to Greavsie, DON'T re-examine his statistics with chairman Irving Scholar. It will only end in tears.

DON'T, unless absolutely necessary, turn up at a club without making an appointment. Invariably, however, managers and players will make themselves available to the *Saint and Greavsie* programme, even at personal inconvenience, and we thank them all for their splendid cooperation.

DO be careful of the producer's unswerving belief that all foreign footballers do speak some English. He has been proved right by the marvellous responses of international stars like Michel Platini, Michael Laudrup, Jan Ceulemans and Harald Schumacher. But his assurances that Enzo Francescoli was also something of a linguist were not shared by the brilliant Uruguayan himself. Despite intensive coaching from one of our editorial team, Jim Ramsey, Enzo couldn't even manage 'I am very happy here in Paris with Racing Club.'

DO also remember that you are given only a certain length of time for your report: rarely more than three minutes, usually two and a half minutes. It is very tempting to ask the subject of the interview about his memories of either the Saint or Greavsie or both. This creates a major problem. The recollections are often the best part of the interview and if included in the final product you can be left with some 20 seconds in which to discuss the burning issue which sent you on your travels in the first place.

Reminiscences about Greavsie usually fall into two categories: those about his phenomenal ability to conjure time and space in the most congested penalty area, and those, like Harry Redknapp's, about his phenomenal staying power in the pub. Either way the stories have all the colour of legend.

The Saint's opponents also remember vividly the quality of his football, along with an occasional explosion of temper which is more likely to surface these days on the golf course when he fluffs a shot!

Of course, we reporters are the straight men to the two characters in the studio. The role is similar to Bernie Winters' dog. Behave yourself and leave the laughs to the entertainers! Joking apart, it is a very rewarding job, although it has its hairy moments. ...

Like timing an introduction to camera on Crewe Station as an express thunders past behind you – knowing that if you fluff your lines the next similar through-train isn't due for another three hours!...

Like being sent to meet Jim McLean for the first time and being told you must make the tough Dundee United boss smile into the lens. (NB Although his players will find this hard to believe, it was not difficult.)...

Like standing on the Newcastle pitch conducting a post-match interview at 10.00 p.m. and receiving a message that you're required at Bournemouth at 9.30 a.m. the next morning. (NB It is possible, too, thanks to the Newcastle–Kings Cross sleeper and a fast car down the M3 and M27.)...

Like persuading Norman Whiteside and David Speedie to talk about their disciplinary records.... Like having to talk to Tottenham and Coventry about their Cup Final records.... Like looking up records of stocks and shares for an interview with potential financier Gary Mabbutt. ...

I always warn the players and managers that the Saint and Greavsie always have the last word. Their part of the programme is always live whereas the reports are usually recorded. Chelsea's Pat Nevin and Neil Webb of Nottingham Forest are among many who come to mind who were sitting in team hotels the Saturday after I'd interviewed them, praying that the studio comment would not be too 'mickey-taking'.. Pat, a genuine individual off the field as

well as on it, duly had his taste in contemporary music mocked. Neil escaped with a kindly remark about his youthful looks in relation to the birth of his first child on the very morning of that particular programme.

The reporters are not immune from sarcastic comment either. Jim's love of sunshine breaks hasn't escaped Greavsie. Nor has Brackers' idiosyncratic dress sense. Nor has my obsession with travelling vast distances to watch matches not always of vast importance.

As you might have gathered, the most important quality for anybody in the entire *Saint and Greavsie* team is a sense of fun. And we all hope that that shines through in the end product.

If you fancy a crack at the job, let me leave you with one final thought. Check that your loved ones have an understanding nature. The hours are wholly unpredictable. Ask my wife Paula. We got married on a Friday morning in March at 11.30 a.m. By 4.00 p.m. I was back in the *Saint and Greavsie* office....

Peter Brackley

Peter Brackley is recognized as one of ITV Sport's most versatile performers.

A World Cup commentator with ITV in Mexico, Peter, who learned his trade in radio, has also made his mark as a presenter and reporter on television. 'Brackers' is also one of Britain's best after-dinner speakers – his amazing range of sporting impressions (including Greavsie) making him a natural attraction for major sporting events.

In this feature he looks back on some memorable moments in his career.

I know it always sounds an exaggeration, but I had ambitions to become a sports reporter, and in particular a football commentator, at the age of eight! I used to

Peter Brackley

practise in my bedroom – commentating on imaginary players in imaginary matches, dreaming of the day I might have the opportunity to cover sporting events for real. That opportunity came my way some 10 years later – a chap called Desmond Lynam, who apparently still features in sports broadcasting on some other channel, was leaving BBC Radio Brighton and freelance replacements were being sought to help form a new sports department. Raw on radio experience but brimming with the enthusiasm generated from a couple of years as a junior news reporter on a local newspaper, I readily took up the challenge – eager to prove my worth. In technical matters, though, I was – and still am – positively useless, and I completely ruined my initial assignment by trailing behind me the tape from the machine in which I had recorded my first interview. Not too much of the conversation was left by the time I had unravelled the tape!

I remember vividly, too, from my early broadcasting days an occasion when I was reporting for local radio on one of Brighton's home games at the Goldstone Ground.

Our 'studio' was a small, glass-fronted hut positioned half-way up the terrace and I was happily chuntering on about Brighton's brilliant play (well, you had to be a little biased on local radio), when one of the less-cultured defenders on view hoisted his clearance loftily and somewhat hastily into the afternoon sky.

'What an extraordinary clearance,' I observed. 'It's so high I've lost sight of it.'

Clearly my colleagues in the commentary hut hadn't. They were cowering on the floor as the ball flew through the window, sending glass in every direction as I informed my audience, amidst much laughter from the others, 'Er ... throw-in to Fulham!'

But then, commentating on football matches will always be a hazardous profession. I once lost my copiously compiled research notes during a game – a strong gust of wind blew them from the commentary gantry down into the packed crowd below, where an elderly gentleman and his friends were perusing them with a mixture of bewilderment and amusement. And I recall, too, the time when a local radio colleague actually missed a goal when he was obliged to stand up to allow a spectator through to his seat! All of us are guilty of verbal slips, too, of course: 'There's grass on the pitch!' I once exclaimed after a bottle had been thrown at Derby's ground. And there are always pitfalls to be encountered in endeavouring to identify players, especially when they have names like internationals Dziekanowski, Mlynarczyk, Bouyahiaoui or Cho Young-Jeung!

But for all its difficulties, sports commentating offers an exciting and rewarding career with many opportunities to travel the world and enjoy memorable sporting occasions. Covering the World Cup finals in Mexico last year was certainly an intriguing experience. The numerous technical problems we faced early on were a major obstacle and for me it was most frustrating to spend the first 'live' match broadcasting only to my co-commentator Ron Atkinson, as no one back home in England could hear a word we were saying! For some inexplicable

reason, all the media seats in the fabulous Jalisco Stadium in Guadalajara had been changed at the last minute and contributions of more than 70 commentators from around the globe were being relayed to the wrong countries! It was most disconcerting to discover this at half-time, although, apparently, I have now a very large following in Sierra Leone!

Covering the finals for the first time as a television commentator, though, was a fascinating assignment and I shall always treasure the memory of the incredible atmosphere in the awesome and so-impressive Azteca Stadium, and the sight of Diego Maradona mesmerizing defenders in the inimitable fashion that captivated us all as Argentina swept to their World Cup triumph. Is Maradona a greater player than Pele was at his peak? Well, I was only fortunate enough to have seen Pele play on a handful of occasions so it is hard for me to judge. But it is equally difficult to believe that anyone can have bettered the mercurial Maradona, whose genius was so perfectly reflected in his stunning goal against England (the second one not the first!). When I returned home from Mexico, incidentally, I discovered my 9-year-old son had now developed a healthy interest in the game. Whether he had yet picked up the rules was not so clear ... in his considered opinion Maradona's goal, which you will remember had left umpteen defenders trailing in his wake, was offside!

For me, though, while Maradona was the outstanding player in the tournament, the most unforgettable match was the quarter-final in Guadalajara – Brazil's defeat by France. It was a classic encounter, with such talented players as Platini, Tigana, Josimar and Careca thrilling the crowd with their exciting skills. What a pity the contest had to be decided on penalties; it was a game neither side deserved to lose. I will cherish fond memories, too, of the fanatical Brazilian supporters and the carnival atmosphere that accompanied their matches at the Jalisco – the constant beat of the famous South American drums, the huge, colourful banners draped over the terracing (one we were told was 100 metres long!), and the sheer bedlam in the streets around the stadium as the fans danced and sang to celebrate their team's early victories in the group matches against Spain, Algeria and Northern Ireland.

Football reporting has given me the chance, too, to meet and work alongside some of the game's outstanding names from the past ... boyhood heroes like Greavsie, Denis Law and Frank McLintock have all become friends and colleagues in recent years on radio and television. And for any youngsters who, like me, have had to relinquish hopes of becoming a professional footballer through lack of ability, I can thoroughly recommend the life of a sports broadcaster as a most acceptable alternative.

8

Scotland ... an open letter

Ian Archer

Ian Archer is one of Scotland's most respected sports journalists. Ian has covered every Scotland World Cup tie since 1974 in West Germany and he has combined his humorous writing skills with regular appearances on Scottish Television as presenter and reporter. He has also become known as Saint and Greavsie's man in Scotland. And in this open letter to Ian and Jimmy he reminds them of the perils of appearing with them.

Dear Saint and Greavsie

I was standing one Saturday lunchtime having a drink in my favourite cocktail bar in Glasgow. It's called the Arlington, in Woodlands Road. In our city a cocktail bar is any boozer which has wall-to-wall sawdust. Actually, the Arlington should be included in any guided tour of Glasgow because its patrons top the bill in that great cast of Scottish football supporters. They know it all – and aren't afraid to express their opinions.

Suddenly, your faces appear on the TV screen. 'Couple of mugs,' says the man on my right, which is the Glaswegian way of telling you that they like you. I couldn't possibly repeat what they say when Jimmy Hill pops up on the other channel. ... And, lo and behold, another crumpled face appears on the box. It's me, talking about that day's Scottish Cup ties, a piece I had recorded an hour before.

'Hearts *v* Celtic is the day's big match and that could go any way,' I say. 'But I'm sorry about your team Hamilton Accies, Greavsie, because they are due to get a football lesson from Rangers.' This statement has an instant effect on my well-being. The Arlington is packed with Rangers supporters and I am now deluged by gold-looking medicine in small glasses. I will need to take a taxi to the game.

If there was a National Society for the Prevention of Cruelty to Footballers, the Accies would never have been allowed near Ibrox. It was a bigger mismatch than Tyson *v* Torvill and Dean, the millionaires against the mugs. Five hours later the *Glasgow Evening Times* had a banner headline saying 'Humiliation' and the secret dairy of Adrian Sprott wasn't secret any more.

Accies had achieved the greatest Scottish Cup triumph since little Berwick Rangers had humbled the mighty Rangers exactly 20 years previously. Twenty-four hours later we were still pinching ourselves to make sure that it had actually happened. How could a side that cost £50,000 to assemble have beaten a team which was worth over £4,000,000? The genie who haunts the Scottish Cup had obviously rubbed it with the red and white of Hamilton.

Accies had hardly won a game all season since being promoted into the Premier Division. Their manager John Lambie had revealed that he wasn't going to get his jollies until the side won a match. In his spare time, he had plenty of opportunity to pursue his hobby – pigeon fancying.

In any case, we were going to Ibrox for an altogether different reason – to watch goalkeeper Chris Woods keep the Accies at bay for 30 minutes and so go a total of 1,196 minutes without conceding a goal to establish a new British record. Chris did it easily and was so unemployed that he could have shaken the hand of every one of the 36,000 crowd and no one would have missed him.

Accies played entirely in their own half. Then, 36 minutes into the second half, they won a free kick in the centre circle. This posed them a problem because no one was prepared to move forward out of their defensive position. What happened is history – full back Adrian Sprott was eventually persuaded to go forward as a one-man expeditionary force, Gerry Collins hit the ball forwards, Rangers' Dave McPherson missed it and the defender hammered the ball passed a startled Woods.

Lambie explained afterwards: 'The chairman told me that if we drew we would have problems with the replay because our floodlights were being repaired. So I told him that we would just have to win it first time.'

You can imagine what the Accies supporters thought of my comments about a football lesson. I kept a very low profile. Back in the Arlington a few days later, the Rangers fans said it was all my fault. Worse still, they insisted that I buy them drinks in return to ease the pain. The next time you ask me to forecast the result of ANY match, I'm going to use that great line from an old Glasgow sports-writer, forced into giving a prediction of how a Rangers *v* Celtic game would finish. 'Only a fool would offer an opinion on the outcome. I confidently state that it will be a draw.'

I've been supporting Scotland for more years than I care to remember, Saint. I can even remember you playing. Always said you looked super in those old baggy pants with the centre parting. I was there on the Hampden Park terraces on 26 September 1961, which wasn't exactly yesterday.

This was the team: Bill Brown; Dave Mackay and Eric Caldow; Pat Crerand, Billy McNeill and Jim Baxter; Alex Scott and John White, yourself, Denis Law and Davie Wilson. We beat Czechoslovakia and you scored a goal. Eventually we lost a qualifying place to the Czechs in a play-off. They went on to be runners up in the World Cup the next year to Brazil and Scotland went nowhere.

I was there in 1974 when we eventually made it to the World Cup in Germany. And onwards to Argentina, which we want to forget, Spain and

Right: *Boss on the ball ... player-manager Graeme Souness, the Anfield old boy who plotted Rangers' rise to the championship and into Europe*

Far right: *Watch out Souness ... Billy McNeill is back in town as Celtic manager in succession to the unlucky Davie Hay*

Above: *Anglo clan ... McRoberts, McWoods and McButcher, Rangers' English international trio, take a bow after a fantastic first season*

Left: *Lone Ranger ... Chris Woods set a British shut-out record before a Hamilton Accies ace Sprotted his copybook*

Mexico. I've travelled a few thousand miles for one of Scotland's goals and I've cried a fair bit along the way.

All that gives me perfect credentials to say that never before have I seen such a poor performance over a season from Scotland than that which was inflicted upon us during 1986–7. The results were dreadful. My honest opinion is that we are at our lowest ebb for 30 years – and that at a time when the club game is booming. So what's gone wrong?

'If the team is winning, then the players get the praise. If it's losing then it's the manager who gets the blame,' said my old pal Tommy Docherty. He's right, and that's put Andy Roxburgh firmly in the firing line.

During the season, Scotland played seven matches, won only one of them – and scored just four goals. Considering that the only win was against the minnows of Luxembourg, you can get a good impression of how low Scotland has sunk. Eire and Brazil won at Hampden Park and Belgium demolished us 4–1 in Belgium. Even the Tartan Army was in tatters.

The truth is that we are going through a bad patch for players, and you can't blame Roxburgh for that. The writing was on the wall in Mexico where we scored only one goal in three games, and Alex Ferguson was responsible for the team then.

It was a controversial decision to appoint Roxburgh, for the last 10 years a highly respected coach of young sides who had even won the European Under-18 Championship. The clever money was on Billy McNeill to get the job. The SFA had different ideas. As secretary Ernie Walker pointed out in his annual report, club managers hadn't exactly set the heather on fire, which was a bit unkind on Willie Ormond and Jock Stein. But he did have a point.

Roxburgh's problems stem from that fact that he hadn't much class material with which to work. No Baxters, no Whites, no Saints, no Laws. When Kenny Dalglish and Graeme Souness made it clear that their careers – at international level – had come to twilight time, he couldn't exactly whistle down the nearest pit and summon up players of their class and experience.

As he led Scotland into the last clutch of meaningless fixtures in the European Championships, Roxburgh was claiming: 'We don't have the skills of former times so it is important that we have a system that everyone understands and every player is prepared to play for each other.' This is a long way from the old days when Scottish flair, trickery and invention were enough to take on the rest of the world, but really he has no choice. Jock Stein said wisely: 'Small countries can't be at the top all the time and we have never managed to play well in both the European Championships and the World Cup.'

But time is running short. The next World Cup is only six months away – and where are we going to find the goalscorers? Answers please on a postcard to Andy Roxburgh c/o SFA, 6 Park Gardens, Glasgow. If you could only lose half a stone, Saint, you could be in line for a comeback.

There's no joke like an old joke – as you know well, Greavsie – and this is one of the oldest. A Rangers fan is putting on his blue and white scarf and heading off for a match at Ibrox. His long-suffering wife looks at him and says: 'I think you prefer Rangers to me.' He looks at her scathingly and replies, 'I'll tell you something, I prefer Celtic to you.'

I've never really believed that could be true, but Rangers supporters have been the butt of a lot of jokes in recent years. 'They spent £12,000,000 creating a new stadium and then found the architect had made a mistake,' says Glasgow comedian Andy Cameron, a Rangers fan. 'They found out that the seats faced the pitch.'

What all this proves is that Rangers in recent years had been a pale shadow of Scotland's most famous and richest club. Not only had Celtic enjoyed the edge on their biggest rivals, but Aberdeen and Dundee United also bested them. They were going nowhere – and fast. Something had to be done – but no one expected the scale of achievement which led to the Rebirth of the Blues.

Rangers have not only been the biggest Scottish football story of the year. They have been the biggest British story as well. Hardly a week has passed without them making big news – and their fans have loved every minute of it. The Accies excepted, of course.

'The biggest compliment I can give them is that this present side looks a lot more like the Rangers side which I used to play in,' says your old sparring partner Jim Baxter. Slim Jim throws praise around like an Aberdonian contributes to charity – so that must be the ultimate accolade.

The story so far ... Rangers shock everyone by appointing Graeme Souness as player–manager. ... He buys three England internationals: Chris Woods, Terry Butcher and Graham Roberts. ... Sell-out crowds take Ibrox attendances to over 1,000,000 . ... And the club end up winning not only the Skol League Cup but also claim their first Championship for nine years.

It was a fairy tale made possible by a recluse millionaire living in

Nevada. Lawrence Marlborough, head of the giant Lawrence building group which has traditionally 'owned' Rangers, decided that the giant club had to rise out of a deep coma. He entrusted the task to his chief executive David Holmes and by applying ambitious business principles, the job was done.

I don't know a soul who thought that Souness would get the job when Jock Wallace packed his bags and ended up in the orange groves of Seville. He was still a successful player for Sampdoria in Italy. But Rangers had noted Kenny Dalglish's success as a player–manager in Liverpool – and looking back the appointment seems so logical.

The arrival of Butcher, Roberts and Woods was even more spectacular. Answering charges that by buying Englishmen he was diluting Scottish football, Souness had the perfect reply: 'We've tried to buy from Scottish clubs, but they talk in telephone numbers. We'll go where we need to get the best players – for this is a club which demands the best.'

For the player–manager his first season was a bitter-sweet experience. He was sent off in the opening match against Hibs and dismissed again when Rangers clinched the Championship at Pittodrie. Let me take you behind the scenes on that day for a cameo which the TV cameras didn't get.

Outside the Pittodrie corridors, the celebrating Rangers fans refuse to leave. Captain Butcher and his team-mates have run constant laps of honour. But Souness, in what should have been his greatest hour of triumph in football, is solemn, almost morose, after his sending off.

'I've let down myself, the club and my wife and family,' he says. He hints that his playing days may be numbered and adds: 'There are certain aspects of the game in Scotland I don't agree with.' And he concludes, 'Rangers will always be physical.' He has set the tone for the years to come.

What Souness has done on the playing front is significant. For years Rangers were the great users of the long ball. They were the cavalry chargers of football, head down, rushing in on other people's goals. When it worked, it was thrilling. When good sides – normally European ones – mopped up these unsophisticated tactics, it was embarrassingly bad.

Souness has brought Anfield tactics to Ibrox. Now there is patient possession football and the Rangers supporters are learning to love it. Their smashing ground – with its 44,000 capacity – isn't big enough to hold the lost legions who have suddenly returned to the colours. For what happened last season, Rangers promise, is only a starter for a period of domination of Scottish football.

Above: *Almost there ... Aberdeen's Jim Leighton (grounded) denies Robert Fleck this time but Rangers are only minutes away from the title*

Above: *Hampden hero ... Davie Cooper weaves his way through Celtic's defence in Rangers' controversial Skol Cup Final victory*

Right: *Jim McLean, whose Dundee United lads reached two cup finals only to lose both, to St Mirren and Gothenburg respectively*

The first trophy, the Skol League Cup, was duly claimed on Sunday, 26 October 1986 against Celtic – a goal from Iain Durrant and a Davie Cooper penalty being enough to beat a Brian McClair effort in an ugly Final. But it showed that Rangers were on their way and the after-match jig of captain Terry Butcher in front of a huge Old Firm crowd showed that he was glad he had made the transition from the sleepy backwater of Ipswich to one of the world's football-maddest cities.

Then there was the long slog throughout the League season as Celtic's lead – once nine points – was whittled away. Finally, the Championship was claimed in Aberdeen and Ibrox celebrated on the last Saturday of the season with a win against St Mirren, with black-market tickets changing hands outside for £50.

It was Rangers' year – and nothing underlined that fact more than when, at the end of the campaign, Celtic sacked Davie Hay and recalled Billy McNeill to the club as manager. Poor nice guy Hay – bulleted because of what Souness had done on the other side of the city.

I went looking for an interview with Jim McLean two hours before the 2nd leg of the Final of the UEFA Cup against Gothenburg. He was calmly sitting in his office dealing with the mountain of mail that had found its way to Dundee United. He looked not to have a care in the world. Later on that evening, he and his side were in tears as the Swedes did the lap of honour with the trophy. But it was still the finest moment of the season because 21,000 Taysiders applauded the victors generously – and UEFA officials looked on approvingly at this British demonstration of sportsmanship.

Sometimes in Scotland we get upset at London's metropolitan arrogance. There was a good case for being angry about the way some parts of the media treated United. The BBC couldn't even pronounce the name of their ground properly.

'We're the corner shop competing with the supermarkets,' said McLean that incredible night when United took on El Tel's millionaires from Barcelona and played them off their Nou Camp pitch. 'We shouldn't really be competing with them.' Goals from John Clark and Iain Ferguson laid that lie in front of the amazed Spaniards.

But McLean had a point. Tannadice gates refused to rise above a steady 7,000 and the club had lost Richard Gough to Spurs for £750,000 before their incredible European campaign began. The point is that the success was similar to Stockport County or Brentford reaching a European final – but in certain quarters south of the border (present company excepted, of course) McLean's men never got the credit they deserved –

even in that horrible space of four days when they lost both the Scottish Cup and the UEFA Cup.

But at least McLean, for so long the solemn po-faced boss who always looked as if he had lost a £1 and found 50p, was suddenly a media star, smiling and relaxed. For 15 years he had struggled to turn United into a club which could challenge the Old Firm in Scotland and the best of the continent abroad.

My mate Jimmy Reid, the former Clydeside sit-in leader, made a good point after St Mirren had taken the Scottish Cup back to Paisley and the town had lined the streets to greet them. 'Coates, the thread people, are the largest employers in the place. Now suppose they had been named as the best exporters in Britain. Would anyone have turned out to cheer the managing director. Of course not. It just shows you how important the football is.'

Especially to Paisley. Since they won the Cup in 1959, the Buddies have had nothing to shout about. Alex Ferguson did revive them as he launched his managerial career, but basically they were also-rans.

That all changed as the Saints took 30,000 to Hampden Park to inflict the first of those two crippling defeats on Dundee United. In truth it was a rather boring final – not a patch on the same day's events at Wembley – at least until extra time. Then Iain Ferguson, a young man who had turned down the chance to go to Liverpool, preferring first-team football at Paisley, put his head down and shot.

'To be honest I never saw the ball go into the net', he told me afterwards. It set off celebrations that lasted throughout the weekend.

It was a triumph for manager Alex Smith, appointed the previous Christmas. An interesting bloke is Alex. He is Billy Bremner's best pal, and has spent his own money travelling round the world to watch four World Cups.

'I promised you a smile if we won,' he said and grinned into the camera. It had been billed as a non-vintage Cup as Rangers, Celtic, Aberdeen and Hearts had all gone out. But that wasn't the way they saw it in Paisley and Hampden's 51,000 crowd agreed.

So it's been a fabulous year for Scottish football. League gates topped 4,000,000 for the first time since the game's halcyon days. That's 80 per cent of the total population of the country. Unlike England, we have no hooligan problem, touch wood. So, you two, if you're searching around for good news stories, look north. And by the way, Greavsie, we're going to give you lot a terrible beating at Wembley. Have fun.

9

Test your knowledge with the Saint and Greavsie sports quiz

Compiled by Chris Rhys

1. If you were performing a ball-out, in what sport would you be competing?
   (*a*) Trampolining
   (*b*) Gymnastics
   (*c*) Croquet

2. Why was world champion Terry Marsh disqualified in May 1987?

3. Sixty-four-year-old 'Pop' Shortell was voted the 1987 USA Sports Nut of the Year. To achieve the honour did he:
   (*a*) Attend a baseball game every day of the season
   (*b*) Record the highlights of ice hockey matches, and edit out the play, but leave in the fights
   (*c*) Referee 11 basketball games in one day

4. How many hoops are there on a croquet lawn?

5. If the Cherry & Whites were playing the Wires, which two famous Rugby League teams would be in opposition?

6. If a team scored two tries, one penalty, one conversion, and a drop goal in Rugby Union, how many points would they score?

7. If a team scored the same in Rugby League, how many points would *they* score?

8. Right, Greavsie … were the Saint's three Football League clubs, in correct order:
   (*a*) Liverpool-Tranmere-Coventry
   (*b*) Liverpool-Coventry-Portsmouth
   (*c*) Liverpool-Coventry-Tranmere

9. OK Saint … see what you remember about Greavsie: were his four clubs, in correct order:
   (*a*) Chelsea–Milan–Spurs–West Ham
   (*b*) Spurs–Milan–Chelsea–West Ham
   (*c*) Chelsea–Spurs–Milan–West Ham

10 In what sport are there five pieces of wood at each end of a chain?

11. On which course did Tony Jacklin have his British Open success in 1969?

12. What unique distinction did Russian tennis player Andrei Chesnokov hold in 1987?
   (*a*) He was the only amateur player ranked in the top 20
   (*b*) He was the only male player in the world top 200 coached by a woman
   (*c*) He used to be a woman!

13. The next is a geography and sports question. There are four English counties that begin with the letter N. Two of them are first-class cricket counties and two are minor counties. Name the latter two.

14. How many spots are on a complete set of double-six dominoes?
    (a) 136
    (b) More than 136
    (c) Less than 136

15. Alphabetically, York City is the last club in the Football League. Which is the next to last?

16. Put the following in the correct order according to which has won the FA Cup the most times:
    Everton
    Liverpool
    Manchester United

17. If Harper became London, Cream became Walcott, and Smith became Robinson, what did Mendeloff become?

18. Every how many years is the Ryder Cup contested?

19 Who was the last Briton to win a Wimbledon title before Jo Durie and Jeremy Bates in 1987?
    (a) John Lloyd
    (b) Anne Jones
    (c) Virginia Wade

20. What was Cassius Clay's middle name?
    (a) Michaelmas
    (b) Marcellus
    (c) Marvellous

21. What is Greg Norman's nickname?

22. Which of the following is *not* a member of the Barry Hearn Matchroom Stable?

    (a) Jimmy White
    (b) Cliff Thorburn
    (c) Willie Thorne

23. Which was the last club Emlyn Hughes led out at Wembley?

24. In boxing, what is a southpaw?

25. The world long jump record as at 1 January 1987 was 29ft 2½in. Within three inches either way, what was it on 1 January 1977?

26. What happened to jockey Stephen Smith-Eccles on the eve of the 1986 Grand National?
    (a) He was kidnapped
    (b) He broke a foot, but still raced and came second
    (c) Disguised as Lady Godiva he rode Red Rum through the streets of Southport

27. What unique feat did Manchester City goalkeeper Eric Nixon perform before Christmas 1986?
    (a) He played in the Rugby League and Football League on successive days
    (b) He played in all City's games up to Christmas, but *not one* was in goal
    (c) He appeared in all four divisions of the Football League between the start of the season and Christmas

28. In the fifth set at Wimbledon does the tie-break come in at:
    (a) 6–6
    (b) 9–9
    (c) Not at all

29. How can you get a 155 break in snooker?

30. When he's in he wears a hard cap but when he's out he wears a soft one. His hitting implement can be made of wood or aluminium. Name the sport.

10

Maybe it's because I'm a Londoner

Jimmy Greaves

There's a spring in the step of ordinary Londoners which I haven't seen for ages. And the reason? At last their football teams are winning again and suddenly London is alive with the buzz which hits the city each time its sleeping soccer giants awake.

Spurs are clicking again – and I don't just mean their turnstiles ... Arsenal are trophy winners ... the Hammers are shining, and even little clubs, such as Wimbledon, seem to be going places. The fans are flocking back, there's fresh, bright young talent bubbling through at every club – and it's marvellous to see.

It was season 1986–7 which set hopes rising that the capital is heading for a revival we haven't really seen since the Gunners' double days 16 years ago. Oh I know that Spurs have won the FA Cup twice in the eighties, but it's the League that counts and to have two contenders in the one city can lift its citizens.

Take Spurs, for instance. Suddenly they are playing fast, attractive, exciting football again. They finished third last year after vainly trying to chase the League, FA Cup and Littlewoods Cup treble. OK, so they came away empty handed, but perhaps Everton would not have had it so easy in the end had David Pleat's men not had to plough their way through a backlog of fixtures.

What leads me to believe that this term Spurs could have their biggest chance in years is the fact that only Everton seem to

be out on their own as an outstanding team. Liverpool to me are not the team they were ... no doubt their new signings will make a difference, but it could take time for Kenny Dalglish to get the blend right and I for one would not be surprised if the Reds have a barren season.

Spurs have played some lovely football over the years, won a couple of trophies, but still haven't a Championship trophy to show for it all since the days of Blanchflower, Mackay and company. This, though, could be their year, for the talent is there. And if David Pleat can find the right man to play alongside Clive Allen up front, then look out Everton.

Spurs last season were, at times, a joy to watch, although too often for my liking Gary Mabbutt and Richard Gough got caught cold with opposition crosses. Still, they both have great talent and perhaps now that David Pleat has bought Chris Fairclough, a natural central defender, from Nottingham Forest, he will switch Richard back to the position he was in when he bought him from Dundee United – right back. Then we might see a great Spurs captain rather than a good one. If that happened, Mabbutt, that versatile little workhorse, would need a new partner at the back ... but surely Spurs must afford that if they want to win a title. Terry Butcher to my mind would have been the ideal choice but as everyone knows he is now doing rather well in chilly Jockoland with Rangers.

But I'm nit-picking. Spurs have a good 'keeper in Ray Clemence. He's still one of the best around and although the midfield system has been changed with the loss of Hoddle, perhaps that is no bad thing. At times Spurs seemed to rely too much on Glenn's skills to get them through. Now

everyone is having to put his best boot forward ... and the new formation is still an exciting one to watch.

I felt sorry for Spurs last term. To be so close to all three trophies and come away empty handed was a painful experience. But the Spurs lads should take some consolation that they were the losers in four of the great club matches of the season: the three Littlewoods Cup semi-final ties with Arsenal and the epic Cup Final encounter with Coventry City. Frankly, Spurs should have won the Arsenal ties. To be 2-0 up overall in the 2nd leg at White Hart Lane and allow the young Gunners back in was criminal. And even in the replay, being one up with only eight minutes to go and then lose was inexcusable. But perhaps Arsenal's name was on the Cup – it certainly must have seemed that way to David Pleat.

John Fashanu getting the better of Everton's Trevor Steven in Wimbledon's classy 3-1 win in the FA Cup

Arsenal made a remarkable recovery under George Graham, one that augurs well for the future. Under Don Howe, Arsenal were the team which always promised but delivered little. Suddenly under Graham, youth was given its chance and it paid off.

Kids such as Niall Quinn, David Rocastle, Tony Adams and Martin Hayes pushed hard for recognition all season with an exciting brand of attacking soccer – and it sparked some urgency into the likes of Charlie Nicholas and Graham Rix. George Graham admitted way back in the autumn of 1986 that he didn't expect his youngsters to stay the course. They didn't, but they still did him proud, leading the First Division for so long. And of course, there was then the bonus of the Littlewoods Cup. Outside Merseyside, I'm certain no true football fan begrudged them their 2–1 win over Liverpool at Wembley in the Final.

Mind you, who would have given tuppence for their chances when Liverpool were giving them the runaround in that first half, particularly after Ian Rush scored the opener. After all, the legend is that every time Rush scored Liverpool were never beaten. Well, beaten they were, by those two Charlie Nicholas goals (Charlie – how could you claim that winner? – it was an oggie if ever I saw one!) and in the end Arsenal deserved the silverware.

That win did enough to convince me that Arsenal under George Graham are on their way back. Their fans have been intensely loyal over the years. Now they must not be too greedy. Give Arsenal time and they will be up there challenging for the title, too.

And what about the Happy Hammers? Well, I'll let you into a secret ... if there's one club I'd love to see win the League, it is the club I finished my senior career with. For West Ham to me epitomize everything that is right in football. Over the years they have played attractive football, been superbly managed and have shown the rest of English football exactly how to conduct their business.

It's worth remembering that the Hammers have never bought a big star. Bobby Moore, Martin Peters and Geoff Hurst were all there as lads, as were Trevor Brooking and my old mate Billy Bonds. In fact, the most money they've ever laid out was that £700,000 they paid for Stuart Robson from Arsenal last season, and that could turn out to be money well spent.

And they've been right when you think of it. While other clubs are still recovering from those madcap days when players who couldn't kick a ball across a room were going for a million pounds, the Hammers stood by their principles and refused to join the transfer merry-go-round. They lived within their means, maintained their reputation and continued to grow their own stars – little Tony Cottee is the prime example of the latest in a long line of home-grown talent. The question is: are they ambitious enough to win a title?

At times, I feel that if someone offered the Hammers board fourth spot in the League and a good run in both Cups every season they'd bite his hand off. They've never quite been able to go for gold ... yet they came close two seasons ago when only a backlog of fixtures wore them down as Liverpool lifted the title.

Certainly the Hammers have the talent to make their mark. Robson will add fire to their midfield, and through the middle of their defence Phil Parkes and Alvin Martin are amongst the best in the business. George Parris is one of the brightest young full backs in British football and up front, if Cottee stays, I expect to see him and Frank

Right: *EastEnders' star ... Alvin Martin shows the iron will that has helped to make West Ham a Cockney success story in the eighties*

Below: *Spur to success ... Gary Mabbutt's commitment has rubbed off on his Tottenham team-mates although Coventry had the last laugh this time*

Below: *Nerve-wracking ... Lennie Lawrence watches anxiously as Charlton battle for survival but he was smiling after his team held off Leeds*

Right: *Flying Fash ... Wimbledon have scored against Southampton, and John Fashanu (left) and Carlton Fairweather are on a higher plane*

Below: *Arsenal's darling ... Charlie Nicholas puts on the style in the Littlewoods Cup Final*

McAvennie snapping back into the scoring routine of two seasons ago. And in young Mark Ward they have one of the bravest, most direct wingers in the game. Put that lot together with one or two more shrewd John Lyall signings and the title would not be beyond them. As I say, all it needs is a bit of ambition ... the skills are there.

Talking about London success stories in 1986-7 – what about Wimbledon? The team from the Southern League who topped the First Division? I used to live in a flat overlooking the pitch at Plough Lane. It was our first home in married life, so the Dons hold a special interest for me. And for a time last season they held the whole of London spellbound with their exploits under the irrepressible Dave Bassett. Football sages all over the country shook their heads in disbelief as they pulled off victories over such as Everton, Liverpool and Manchester United – and to finish in sixth position as they did was absolutely fantastic in their first season up.

Now under new management, it remains to be seen whether they can stay up, but even if they don't, they have added fun to London football life. Sure, they were a little rough and ready – but their happy, almost amateur, outlook must have shaken the dismal Johnnies who believe football should be all work and no play.

And didn't John Fashanu leave his mark? Fash the Bash is not exactly the most cultured player I've ever seen, but he made some of the big international defenders work for their money. And despite criticisms, Wimbledon weren't just an up-and-at-'em outfit. Anyone who watched their classic Cup tie against Everton where they stuffed the champs 3-1 will remember the likes of Kevin Gage and Glyn Hodges playing football of the highest quality.

There's talk of Wimbledon moving elsewhere, but I hope it never happens. The Wimbledon fans are amongst the friendliest in London, they've followed their club from Fourth Division right through to First. It would be a shame to take those smiles off their faces, Mr Hamman.

As I say, season 1986-7 was a good one for the London clubs, but while Messrs Graham, Pleat and Bassett were the idols of the media, my manager of the year was not amongst that trio. My own favourite was Lennie Lawrence of Charlton Athletic. For what a job Lennie did in keeping Charlton in the First Division. I know it took until the very last minute of the season by gaining an extra-time play-off win over Leeds United, but the fact that Athletic got to that stage at all was a miracle.

Let's face it, who'd fancy the chances of a club who three years ago were facing the receiver, don't have a ground of their own, and had to make do with gates of only 6,000? Yet Lawrence, with some shrewd buying and selling, kept Athletic alive in the First and so paid back the fans who travelled from the Valley to Crystal Palace. And yes, Saint, I know their Scottish striker Jim Melrose did his bit!

And what about Chelsea, the club I cut my senior teeth on? Well, money doesn't seem to be the problem these days. The close-season signing of Clive Wilson and Tony Dorigo were excellent buys, but there's something wrong with the old club and it's difficult to put the finger on what.

And who can blame the Chelsea fans for not exactly being as cheerful as normal? For the past two seasons the club has been in turmoil. Players wanting out, talk of dressing-room revolts ... the 'All the best' club of my youth has been in serious disarray and I cannot see things improving